D0991596

Chinese Brush Painting

A Practical Guide

Chinese Brush Painting

A Practical Guide

Joseph Chan

TIMES EDITIONS

I am grateful for the appreciation and support of my family and friends, especially my daughters Mary Sun and Joan Lowcock, without whose encouragement this book would never have seen the light of day.

Chinese Brush Painting
is published by
Times Editions Pte Ltd
an imprint of Times Editions Pte Ltd
Times Centre, 1 New Industrial Road
Singapore 1953

Printed in Singapore by Kim Hup Lee Printing Co. Pte Ltd

ISBN 981 204 075 7

CONTENTS

雪壓銀梢

FOREWORD

This book is a practical manual for the acquisition of essential skills in the art of Chinese painting. It is designed for people interested in learning the creative process of one of the oldest art forms in the world. In Chinese it would be known as the beginner's primer to open the "entrance door" to advanced technical knowledge.

The object of this book therefore is both to help the reader attain a degree of technical proficiency and to lay the groundwork for the development of a *reasoning* mentality so that, in time, the student would become his or her own teacher.

The resolution of technical problems, the difficulties they present to the uninitiated, and the common cause of such hindrances, are arranged to allow an exploratory examination of ways to deal with them. Having been informed of the cause and effect of the problems beforehand, the novice will be able to scrutinize them with circumspection, and develop the ability to perceive and understand the whys and wherefores of these difficulties as they arise.

The delicate hand or wrist actions are so intricate that mere words are inadequate to provide precise description of the physical process involved. A more direct method is to compare these manipulations to similar motions routinely performed by a person in his daily activities. Once the student realizes he is on familiar turf, he becomes instantly relaxed and his response is generally enthusiastic. It is particularly effective for class instruction.

My experience as a teacher of Chinese painting tells me that, though the number of people interested in the practice of the art has been steadily increasing in recent years, it has nevertheless a long way to go before attaining the level of popularity that Chinese "wok" cooking currently enjoys worldwide. In my opinion, it is not for want of interest in the art; it is because of the dearth of informative manuals that Chinese brush painting remains in this state of relative obscurity.

The love of art in any form is an expression of profound personal predilections; and the development of art thrives only in the soil of popular acceptance.

Take for instance the development of the Western arts in recent history. Without the multitude of dedicated music lovers, the knowledgeable patrons who have studied music and who form the main body of concertgoers among teachers, doctors, lawyers, engineers, accountants, housewives, bakers and others, without the grassroots support of all the armchair musicians in the world, it would indeed be difficult to visualize the grand concert halls of the modern age with their huge seating capacity—quite unthinkable indeed in the time of Beethoven, Brahms or Tchaikovsky.

The purpose of this book therefore is to meet the general need for illustrated manuals especially designed to provide essential information on the practical art of Chinese painting.

Joseph Chan
January 1991

INTRODUCTION

A Historical Review of Chinese Brush Painting

Painting as a form of art in China goes back to remote antiquity, as shown by the records that have survived to this day. The work of chronicling had become an established occupation after the age of the sage Confucius. Since then only human frailty and political upheaval have prevented the facts of an era from reaching the hands of later historians, such as the wholesale burning of classical books under Emperor Qin Shih Huang Di of the Qin dynasty (221–206 B.C.), builder of the Great Wall of China. This left a cultural void of several centuries in the annals of ancient China.

The earliest contact with Indian Buddhism in China is believed to have taken place after Emperor Wu of the Han dynasty (206 B.C.–A.D. 220) dispatched his expeditionary forces to explore the far west over difficult terrain inaccessible to ordinary travelers. The tracks established by his armies were later turned into caravan routes used by traders to travel overland to China in quest of silk, a commodity much in demand in countries west of the border. As business prospered and traffic increased, other travelers, including clergy from India, followed; the rest is history.

If the coming of Buddhism had left a mark on Chinese culture, its impact was not always visible in the mundane day-to-day lives of the people: by the next prosperous Song (A.D. 960–1279) period, the Bodhisattva of Infinite Mercy had assumed Chinese features in paintings and religious statues; taken a Chinese name, Guan Yin; and been replaced by a female physical form. That the transformation of his physical appearance had not affected the faith of Guan Yin's worshipers bears testimony to the eclectic pragmatism of Chinese culture, including the one branch that has always been the pride of the Chinese people—the art of brush painting.

Gu Kai-Zhi (A.D. 346–407), a gifted painter of religious figures* and renowned "father of traditional landscape painting,"

* The *Li Tai Ming Hua Zhi* (*Record of Famous Paintings of Past Dynasties*) records that Gu became an overnight success after people saw the huge picture of the Buddha he had painted on one wall of a Buddhist temple.

was also well-known for his exquisite paintings of boats, bamboo shoots and ducks. Gu's artistry as an outstanding painter of human figures can be seen from copies of his works which exist in the collection of the British Museum, London, and the Palace Museum, Taipei.

Peace and prosperity during the early part of the Tang dynasty (A.D. 618–907) set the stage for the most fruitful period in Chinese cultural development. If art is the barometer of the general well-being of a nation, then the greatness of the Tang era may be seen in its incomparable vigor, nobility of form and seemingly unlimited capacity for growth in diverse directions.

Apart from advances in calligraphy and landscape painting, of which many pieces became timeless classics, the painting of birds-and-flowers became accepted as an independent branch of equal importance to the traditional school of landscape painting.

The brief interregnum known as the Five Dynasties (A.D. 906–960) was a prelude to the glorious cultural accomplishment of the Song dynasty. The first ever Academy of Painting was founded during this period, which also saw the prominent successes of four landscape artists—Jing Hao, Guan Tong, Dong Yuan and Li Cheng—whose massive, towering mountain scenes painted with tactile strokes in monochrome ink presaged the emergence of a stylized genre of painting which would be of lasting influence on landscape painting. In the field of birds-and-flowers, Xu Shu, a master of small subjects such as fish and insects, was acclaimed as the father of the "boneless" (see chapter "The Plum") style of painting, a style that has remained one of the most popular motifs down to the present time.

The next period, the Song dynasty (A.D. 960–1279), was a time of cultural expansion of enormous magnitude, the era of the intellectual, the scholar, the poet, and the elevation of aesthetic conceptions to an unprecedented level. The art of painting was to play an extremely vital role.

One important element that aided in the proliferation of a variety of styles in this period was the establishment of a grand Palace Academy of Painting: the best talents of the time were recruited to work under one roof with the sponsorship of Emperor Hui Zong, himself a gifted artist of birds-and-flowers paintings*.

In the Academy, old ideas were scrutinized and new ones explored. This led to a new "Palace" style of painting characterized by meticulous attention to details, delineated with fine, linear brushwork. In a departure from the traditional criterion of assessing the quality of a painting wholly on its external attributes, consideration was also given to the internal or subjective intuition of the "inner mind" of the painter.

The new libertarian concept found ready support among independent gentlemen painters not inhibited by official prescriptions. One of them, Wen Tong (A.D. 1018–1079), the best-known of the bamboo artists, perfected a definitive style parti-

* Copies of his works on human figures and birds-and-flowers exist in the collection of the Boston Museum of Fine Arts and the Palace Museum, Taipei.

cularly suited to the painting of weathered trees, rocks and bamboos that was to characterize Chinese painting through its history.

Wen's contemporary, Su Shih (A.D. 1036 –1101) (also known as Su Dong Bo), outstanding poet and calligrapher and devoted painter of bamboos, was the author of the famous lines: "Would I rather live without meat; but never, O never, without bamboo."

For the arts, the period from 1279 to 1368 was one of the contradistinction between two major trends of thought: that between naturalism and conventionalizing tendencies. The end of the Song dynasty and the enthronement of the nomadic rulers were, right from the beginning, traumatic for the gentry who supported the art of painting. Artists all over the country were split in their reactions to the abrogation of the Academy and the capture of its benefactor, the Emperor Hui Zong.

Zhao Meng Fu (A.D. 1254–1322), brilliant calligrapher and painter of landscapes in ink and color, was among the leading artists to champion the call for the revival of Tang and Song styles, perhaps as a reminder to his compatriots of the past glories of the nation before the fall of the Song dynasty. However, in contrast to the conservatism of this school of thinking, other prominent artists, including the celebrated Four Great Masters of Yuan, took a different approach. To them, the human mind should be sublimated through more harmonious rapport with Nature: the ideal of personality in revolt. It was in fact a reaffirmation of the escapist "inner mind" thinking that had surfaced earlier in the Song era.

One of the Four Masters of Yuan, Wu Zhen (A.D. 1280–1354)*, a devout Confucianist with a profound understanding of Taoist and Buddhist teachings, liked to sign his paintings as "The Plum Tree Taoist." An accomplished calligrapher, he was, like Su Shih before him, a revered artist of paintings of the bamboo which he regarded as an emblem of nobility attainable through calligraphic proficiency.

After the authority of the Mongol rulers collapsed in 1368, Ming Emperor Hong Wu quickly set up an Academy of Art similar to the one founded by the Song dynasty, but of a smaller scale and magnitude.

Centuries of nomadic invasions and internal unrest in the north had turned the temperate and agriculturally productive southern regions into a land of hope and safety for many people. This was especially true of the areas around the rich delta basin along the Sung and Yang Zi rivers on the east coast, where trade and easy access to the outside world also contributed to their prosperity. It is no accident, therefore, that all three leading Ming Schools of Painting took their roots within that region.

Shen Zhou (1427–1509) of Su Zhou, a busy river town near Shanghai on the sea coast, was the best-known of the artists of the Wu (ancient name for Su Zhou) School of Painting. Many of his pupils are now well-known names among eager collectors of Chinese paintings.

* The other three of the Four Great Masters of Yuan were:
Huang Gong Wang (1269–1355), Wang Meng (1301–1385) and Ni Zan (1301–1374).

Besides being the mentor of many illustrious artists, Shen was also one of the most admired literati painters of his time; and it was due in large part to the artistry of his unique style that his group was catapulted to the center of the cultural revival of the Ming dynasty.

Toward the end of the Ming period, the painting of birds-and-flowers of the spontaneous style reached its most natural form in the hand of Shu Wei (1521–1593). His works reflected the best of the great Xie Yi* style with the splashed-ink motif.

Another gifted artist from the same area, Dong Qi Chang (1555–1636), native of a suburb of Greater Shanghai, was a celebrated calligrapher, collector of paintings and art critic. At the height of the creative boom preceding the fall of the Ming dynasty, a critical controversy erupted among the artistic community regarding the comparative styles of the northern and southern great masters. In one of his writings on the subject, *Hua Zhi* (*Painting Principles*), Dong added his weight on the side of the southern artists by asserting that the growing Buddhist Chan (Zen) influence on the works of the Southern School was a positive development complementary with the elevation of the inner mind to attain a state of awareness of the quintessence of Nature. In his opinion, this was the *tour de force* of the acquisition of technical skill in the art of painting.

Unlike in the preceding Ming period, the institution of an academy of painting was discarded by the Manchu rulers. In the absence of an independent bureau to oversee aesthetic affairs, "workers of painting" were hired to paint portraits of members of the Imperial Family and to undertake other decorative works on the palace buildings.

Meanwhile, away from the palace, great strides in the development of the Xie Yi style had culminated in the works of the "survivor artists."** This was characterized by the paintings of four gifted monks:

Hong Ren (1610–1664), great admirer of Ni Zan of the Yuan dynasty, was a remarkable landscapist noted for his paintings of the plum tree and the bamboo in the outlined mode. Without the washes of the Song masters, his landscapes were characterized by their rectilinear form that highlights the spaciousness of his works.

Zhu Da (1626–1705) was one of the best-known artists of his time in China. A gifted poet, calligrapher and prolific painter of landscapes, fishes and birds-and-flowers, he displayed in his works an originality of perception, an intensity of expression and a simplicity of treatment of subject that were totally unprecedented.

Like Zhu Da, Shi Tao (1640–1718) became a monk, spending much of his time traveling and visiting famous mountains and scenic places. A genius with a stupendous technique, he was more balanced and fluent in style than Zhu Da. A remarkable theoretician, he left behind a treatise on the art of painting, *Hua Yu Lu* (*Discourse on Painting*), which has become one of the most widely read works on the subject.

* So named because, as a rule, literati artists were proficient in the art of calligraphy, an essential technique for that type of painting. Thus, the two verbs "write" and "draw" have become synonymous in Chinese artistic jargon.

**These were artists whose loyalty still remained with the vanquished Ming dynasty.

Chronic poor health confined Shi Qi (1617–1689) to the life of a semi-recluse. By nature, he was inclined to be discriminative in his response to demands for his paintings. Thus, only a few of his works are known to be extant. A non-conformist in spirit, he was more concerned with imagery than brushwork manipulations. Perhaps it is because of this that some of his landscapes suggest influences from European prints which were available to Chinese artists from the early seventeenth century.

Not all the best talents of this period were monks though. One of them, Yun Shou Ping (1633–1690), a scholar and calligrapher of exceptional merit, was described as "the greatest painter of birds-and-flowers." His style was so refreshing it was said to have eclipsed all the other conventional styles.

Zheng Xie (1693–1765), creator of a definitive style of calligraphy, is famous for his paintings of the orchid and the bamboo. These two plants often appear together in his works. He was a great admirer of the bamboo, which he believed to have a soul.

Since the beginning of the Qing dynasty, small groups of artists have been identified by critics either by their names, such as "the Four Wangs;" or their residential districts: "The Eight Artists of Jin Ling;" the particular style they shared: "The Eight Eccentrics;" or the areas where they worked: "The Ling Nan School" in the south and "The Shanghai School" in the east. Space does not allow us to address each of them separately in this brief review. That they are known as a distinct group of artists is proof of a degree of excellence *per se*.

Finally, it is fitting to pay tribute to a few of the great masters of living memory who, by their ingenuity and perseverance, have all broken new ground in an age of change and innovation, to become the standard-bearers for a new generation of students of the art of Chinese painting. They are:

Wu Chang Shi	1844–1927
Qi Bai Shi	1863–1957
Gao Jian Fu	1879–1951
Chen Shu Ren	1883–1948
Shu Bei Hong	1863–1957

Fundamentals of Painting

The earliest reference to the group consisting of the orchid, the bamboo, the chrysanthemum and the plum as an independent branch of Chinese painting can be traced back to the Song dynasty. During that era a number of artists, proficient in calligraphy and determined to break away from conventionalized forms of painting, began to explore new thematic subject matter to project their idealistic style. They stressed the importance of rhythmic brushwork and spontaneous expression. Being lovers of nature as well, they found their ideal subjects in these four plants (also known as the Four Paragons).

Owing primarily to the combined and comprehensive range of brushwork technique associated with the painting of the Four Paragons, the latter eventually came to be accepted as the standard model for learning the fundamental skills of the art of painting in China.

Another factor that no doubt contributed to their popularity as technical models for learners of Chinese brush painting is the fact that their growth cycles coincide with the four seasons of the year*. This phenomenon is consistent with the Taoist concept of cosmic harmony of the three quintessential Principles:

Heaven – the four seasons
Man – the ideals of Man
Earth – the soil, Mother Nature, from which all plants grow

However, the order in which the lessons are presented in this book does not follow the seasonal cycles of these four plants. Instead this course is based on the specific type of brushwork required for each particular subject. It is arranged in a progressively graded curriculum geared to developing the technical skill which is needed at each stage.

Briefly, the techniques addressed in each chapter include the following:

Bamboo

As moral emblem:

The strong, flexible stalks of the bamboo symbolize the unyielding integrity of a fine moral character.

Type of brushwork:

Firm, straight lines, and double-loading process.

* Orchid, spring; Bamboo, summer; Chrysanthemum, autumn; and Plum, winter.

Plum

As moral emblem:

The plum's ability to flourish in late winter symbolizes eternal hope and rejuvenation.

Type of brushwork:

Introduction of curved lines, dots and the "boneless" type of petals as well as the outlined model.

Orchid

As moral emblem:

The fragrance of the orchid flower and the long flowing leaves symbolize the grace and refinement of a superior person.

Type of brushwork:

Thin, filmy petals and long, flowing lines executed with extended arm and body actions.

Chrysanthemum

As moral emblem:

Blooming in a variety of forms in autumn, the chrysanthemum symbolizes moral strength and fortitude.

Type of brushwork:

Introducing "boneless" leaves superimposed with sinewy leaf veins and curly petals arranged in circular tiers.

This course is designed for classes of six to eight, and can be completed in 30 to 40 sessions of two to three hours each. The techniques studied here cover the basic skills applicable to most other types of flowers and plants as well.

The best way to explain the exemplary value of the Four Paragons as standard guide models for the student of Chinese brush painting is to quote Wang Zhi, artist and compiler of the famed *Mustard Seed Garden Manual* (1887)*. In this passage, he refers to the unique merits of the Four Paragons:

"*Those plants, the noblest of them all, are truly unique. They represent the* Qi *(breath of life) of the Four Seasons. Is it not therefore fitting, in compiling a manual of this nature, that they should be studied first before all other plants?*"**

* Published in three volumes, the *Mustard Seed Garden Manual* is the first comprehensive, authoritative manual of Chinese painting. The second volume is exclusively devoted to the study of the Four Paragons; the other two volumes deal with such subjects as Critical Essays; Human Figures and Buildings; Flowering Plants and Insects; Birds and Famous Masterpieces; Reproductions of Famous Masterpieces of Rocks; and Trees.

**The above quotation is from Wang Zhi's introductory remarks in the *Book of Chrysanthemums* of the second volume of the *Manual*. Translation by the author.

Equipment and Supplies

If you are taking up the art of Chinese brush painting for the first time, then you need to know all about the essential tools and material supplies that make up the student's standard equipment so that you can begin painting.

Why use black China ink to begin with?
Before the advent of bottled liquid ink, dried ink stick made from pine soot or lamp-black mixed with vegetable oil and gum was the standard medium used in calligraphy and painting in China. Many coloring materials used in the Orient are limpid and have to be mixed with ink to give them body. Thus the black ink stick ground with water in a stone ink-well has always been one of the essential coloring mediums, used in combination with other water colors. Bottled ink is a modern substitute for the sticks and is gaining greater popularity because it takes the toil out of preparing fresh ink every time you sit down to paint.

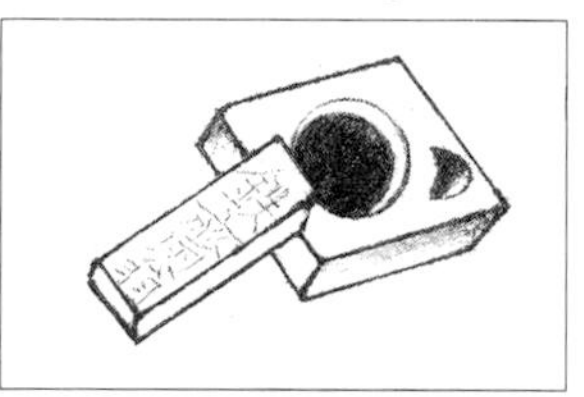

Is "rice paper" really made of rice?
The answer is definitely "No." Regardless of the fact that it is widely known as such in the West, the term is a misnomer. Rice is the staple food in the Orient; it is thus too valuable to be used as raw material for paper-making. In China, many different kinds of materials are used to make paper specially marketed for calligraphy and painting, such as the barks of green sandalwood and mulberry and hemp fibres. While many grades of paper are available, both with regard to quality and thickness, all are handmade to a very fine texture which, together with absorbent quality, are considered most appropriate for Chinese brush painting. The style sets great store on spontaneous ink-play made possible by the natural merging of ink on permeable paper. A subtle spectrum of color tones can be created with a single stroke of the brush.

What then is the role played by the brush in such a style of painting?
Before we examine the role of the brush in Chinese painting, let us go over briefly the

physical parts of the most common types of brushes (see "Parts of the Brush"). Of the three different brushes illustrated, we will be concerned, for now, only with the largest one, called the Medium Orchid-Bamboo brush. At the top of the long handle is a small loop by which the brush is hung to dry when not in use. At the other end is the tuft of animal bristles set into the hollow core of the handle and bonded with glue. The type of semi-soft animal bristles used in the Orchid-Bamboo brush is known as "wolf hair," which may in fact consist of a blend of various kinds of animal hair of different grades of hardness and texture. Generally, a brush is judged by the length and quantity of the bristles in addition to the resilient ability of the hairs at the front of the tuft to retain their shape when released from pressure.

The secret of the hidden reservoir

The contour of the Chinese brush when wet is shaped much like the flame of a glowing candle—wide in the middle where it is packed with bristles but tapered to a fine point at the tip where there are only a few of the longest hairs. Higher up, the "belly" acts as the storage area to retain ink by capillary action even when the brush is held in the upright position. On the other hand, the sharply reduced number of hairs at the tip makes it possible for it to draw an extremely fine line more delicately than any other type of writing instrument and keeps it up for a longer period of time.

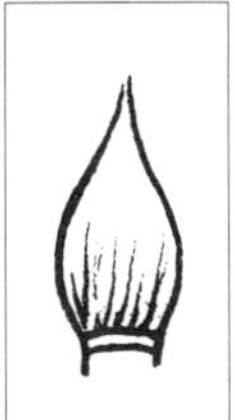

How to break in a new brush

When new, the whole tuft is held together by a gum of low viscosity. In that state it is slim, tight and shaped like the Leaf Vein brush shown in "Parts of the Brush." Therefore, a brand new brush has to be "opened," by gently and repeatedly pressing the front third part of the brush against the side of a cup or bowl filled with clean, warm water. It will take only a moment for the bristles to soften if it is rotated from side to side at the same time. (Eventually, after continued use, the tuft may fill out to look like the larger brush illustrated.) Once removed, the cap that comes with the new brush should be discarded since it is no longer wide enough to accommodate the hairs after the brush has been "opened."

After that, use only cold water to rinse out the brush to protect the gum that bonds the tuft to the handle.

Parts of The Brush

Supplies and Equipment

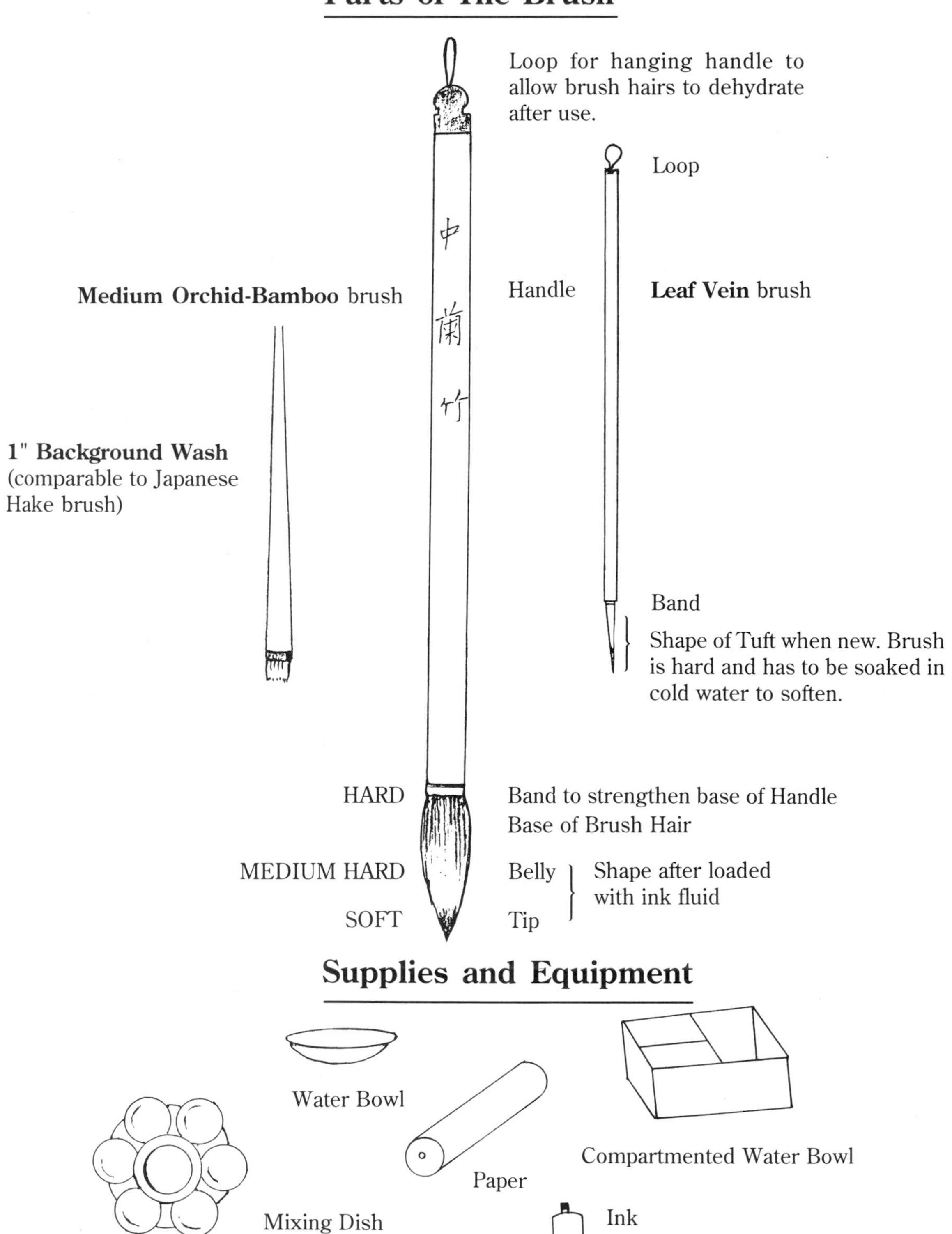

BEGINNING

The standard hand hold and the role of the fingers

You are now ready to pick up the brush to find out how it responds to your directions in the performance of intricate maneuvers used in Chinese painting. However, before your commands can be accurately transformed into action, they must be effectively transmitted to and clearly understood by the brush. A great deal would depend on how the brush is gripped by your hand to steer it in the most effective manner. The following preliminary tests show the kinds of actions taken by the hand and the fingers to set up the standard all-purpose grip used for Chinese brush painting.

Shake hands with the brush

Preliminary Test I

Extend your hand in front of you with all five fingers stretched forward like in a handshake.

Test II

Now bend the last four fingers back in such a way that the first phalanx of the index finger comes to rest against the tip of the thumb, which has to bend down a little to complete the natural shape of the hand gripping something with a hollow palm.

At this point, your hand will be in the same shape as when it is holding a brush in the upright position. Yes, it is as simple as that. And if there are still doubts about the effectiveness of the test because here the hand is empty, there is another simple way to check if the recommended grip is indeed viable in actual practice. The hand hold at the end of the test is basically the same as the natural posture of a person holding up a champagne glass by the stem at social functions. The standard Chinese painting grip is indeed very simple.

The test outlined here only shows how the hand would appear *after* the brush is in hand. What comes before that and the part played by the fingers as individual members of a composite team to hold the brush firmly and securely at all times, is examined in the following section.

The roles and work stations of the fingers

Here is a step-by-step review of the process of executing a right-handed grip:

1. Pick up the handle of the brush with the left hand, with its tip pointing to the right.
2. Place the first phalanges of the index and middle fingers of the right hand on the side facing away from you, about three inches above the base.
3. Next bring the first phalanx of the thumb up against the underside of the handle directly at right angle to the index finger.
4. Then bring the fourth finger up against the underside of the handle, a little to the right of the middle finger. Unlike the other fingers, the fourth finger does not touch the handle with the fleshy part of the phalanx, but with the opposite side instead. The contact point is somewhere between the fingernail and the first

knuckle (see figure presenting "side view" of hand hold under "The Beginner's Brush Hold"). In fact, the knuckle is better as it is more sensitive than flesh.

Thus you have placed two separate sets of "prongs" on the handle. These are formed by the thumb and the index finger working together as the first set of "prongs" and the other two fingers completing the assembly as the second set. For the combined setup to be effective, all the fingers should be slightly curved and the palm hollowed like the inside of a bowl and not in contact with any of the fingers. The little finger should stay as close as possible to the fourth finger for support. Finally, remove your left hand, turning your right wrist in a clockwise direction. You will then be holding the brush in the upright position as shown in Fig. B in the section "Rolling the Handle and Raised Hand in Working Posture."

With the brush now firmly secured in a standard working grip, we can turn our attention to the type of elementary brushwork achieved by the most natural hand and wrist actions.

The Beginner's Brush Hold

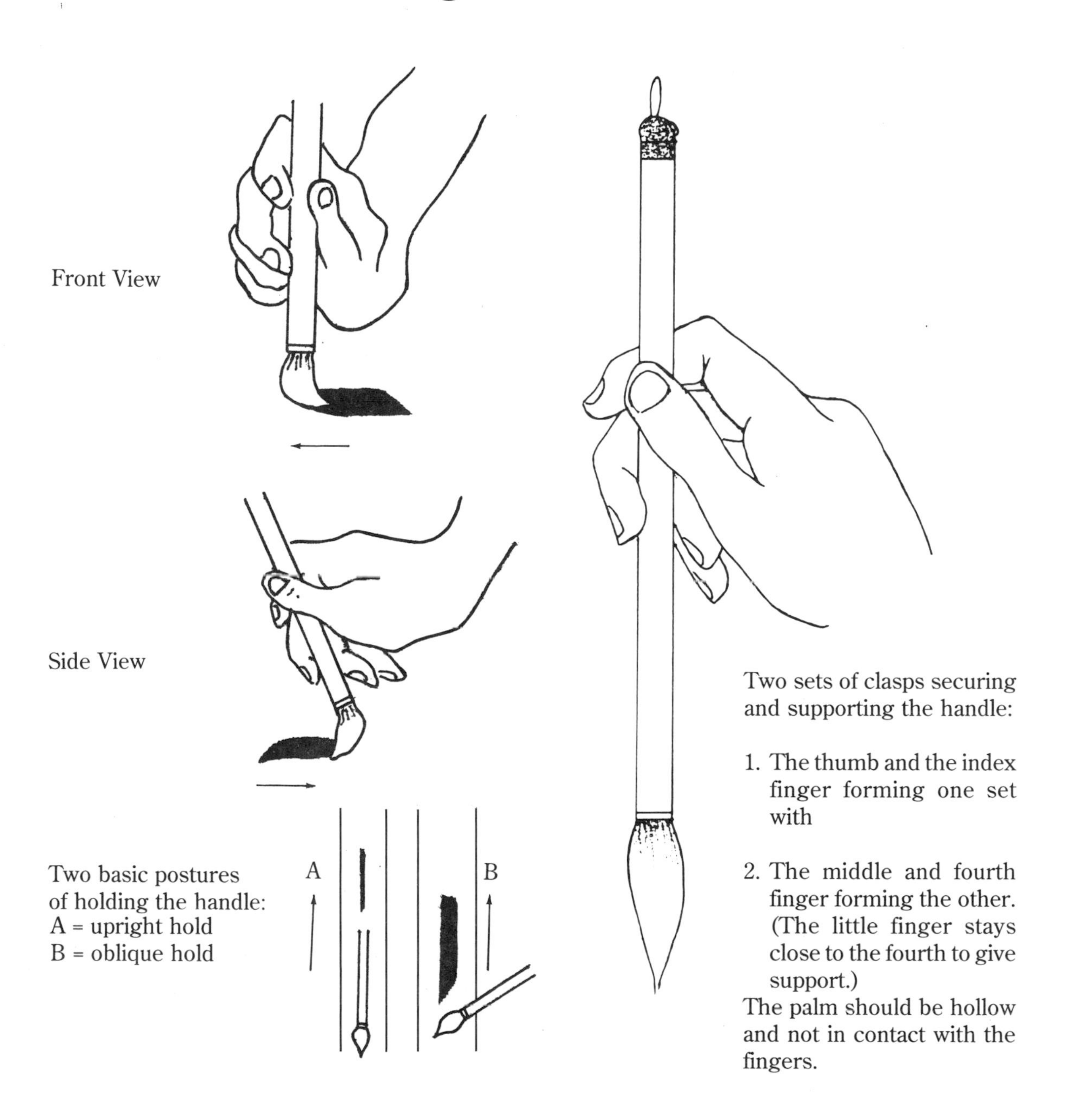

Slim line drawn by the upright hold, wide line by the oblique hold

Rolling the Handle and Raised Hand in Working Posture

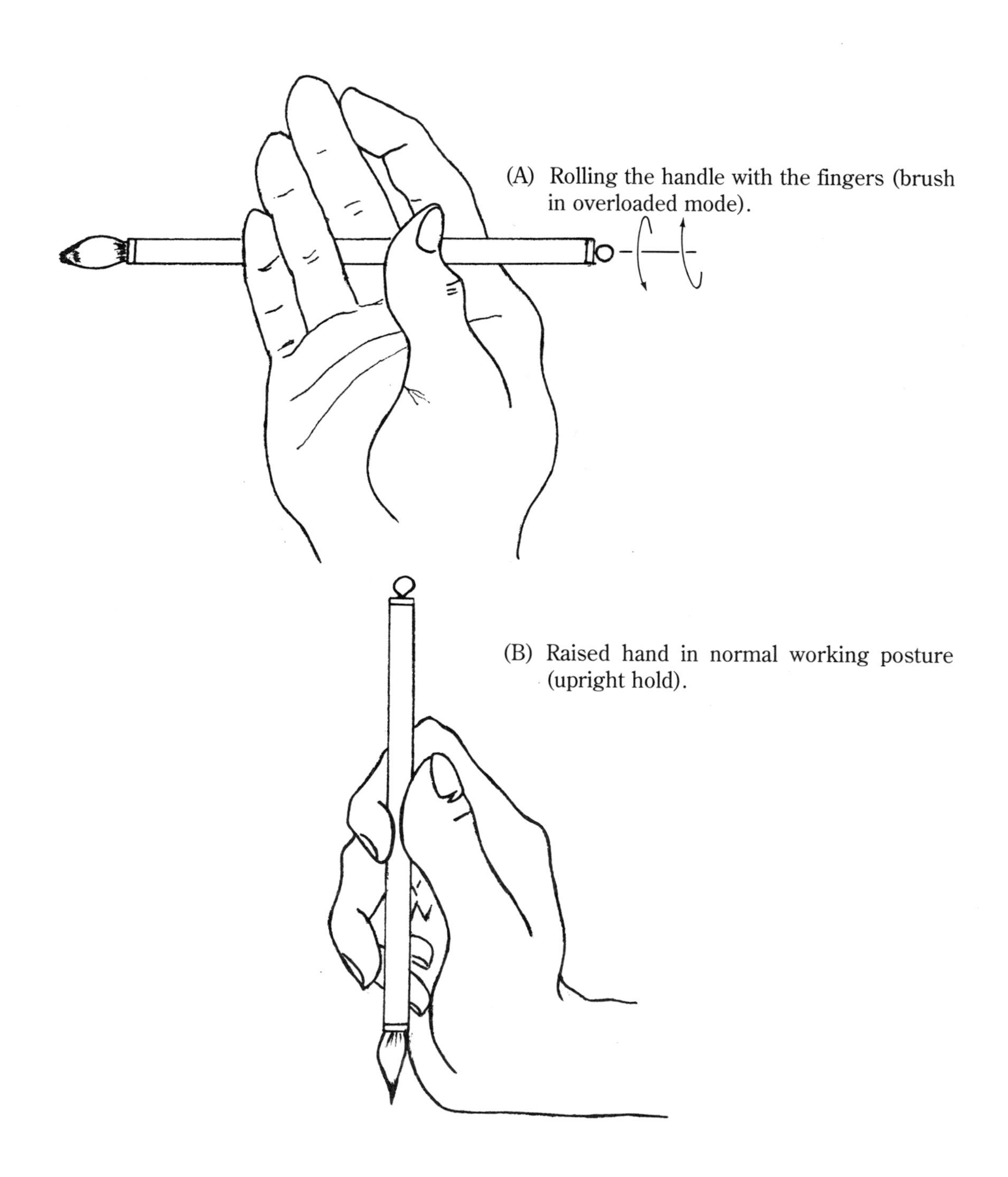

A pendulum in your hand

As Chinese painting is fundamentally a linear art, it is important to determine what physical or mechanical aspects of the movement of the hand or of the brush are involved in the process of executing simple brushwork.

In the previous section, we saw how the brush is raised to the upright position. Now, if the hand is made to turn all the way to the left and back again like in the "doorknob" action detailed later in the "Spindle stroke test exercise," it becomes clear that the handle of the brush will perform in much the same way as that of a pendulum. In this experiment, the brush would only be tracing an arc in the air; yet had the brush been loaded and in contact with a painting surface, it would have traced a well-defined straight line on a piece of paper. In order to form a truly straight line from point A to point B, the hand has much to gain by learning from the working process of the pendulum.

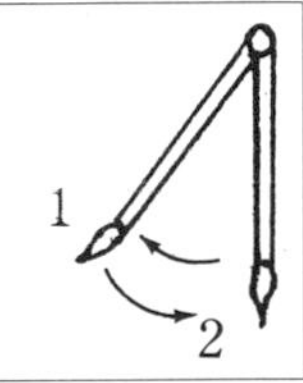

This has only solved part of the problem concerning the way the handle of the brush operates in the upright position. There remains the other half of the problem, the question of the hand itself. Are there any features of the human hand that may affect and nullify the assured, invariable constancy of the motion of a pendulum? Once again, the best way to respond to that question is to go through the pertinent motions in a simple test:

Step I

While holding the brush in the upright position, turn the wrist all the way to the left in the "doorknob" action (or when turning the key to lock a drawer) and return to the original position.

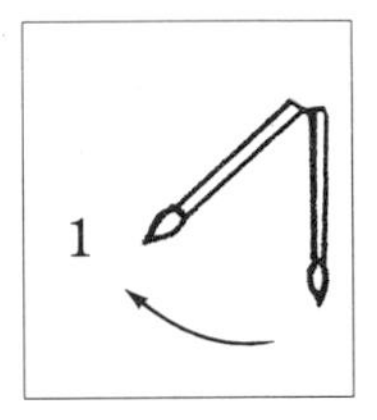

Step II

Repeat the same action but, this time, turn the wrist in the opposite direction; i.e. to the right.

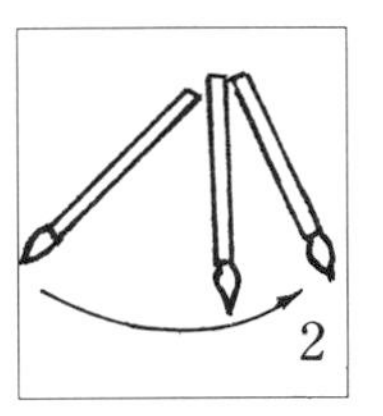

Step III

Combine Step I and Step II to arrive at Step III as shown. (Note that the above test is carried out with the brush not yet loaded with ink.)

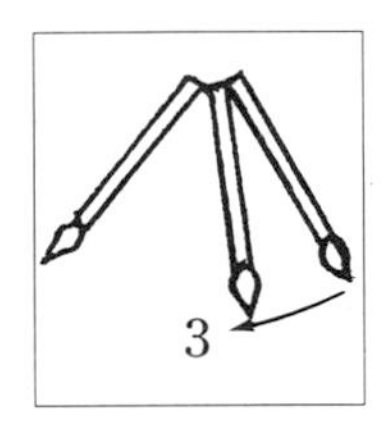

The result of the above test bears out the important fact that, during the movement to the left (Step I), the brush traces a much wider arc than the distance covered by Step II while moving to the right. The human wrist is so structured that, on a right-handed person, the ability to rotate the hand to the right with the elbow anchored in a fixed position, is noticeably more restricted than turning in the other direction. Because of this unevenness in the rotative range of the human wrist, there has been a call to divide Chinese brush strokes into two broad categories, namely: (1) "smooth" or unhindered strokes and (2) "restricted" or more precisely "against the grain" strokes (as they say in Chinese). Other types of physical hindrances will be addressed later in this book.

Checks and balances of the fingers

Positioned at the top of the assembly to function as the primary hinge of a pendulum swing, the thumb and the index finger, the strongest of the group, are also responsible for tilting the brush up and down or sideways whenever it is needed, shortly before the wrist, the primary source of motive power, is activated. The index finger, the weaker partner, has to make a conscientious effort to exert a check on the forward thrust of the thumb working from the opposite direction. This is a prime condition for the development of a firm hold of the brush with these two fingers working as a team.

The same rule applies to the other two fingers, with special attention focusing on the ability of the weaker one to provide an effective counterbalance against the stronger finger.

The special functions of the second set of fingers

Notwithstanding the fact that the middle and fourth fingers are the weaker members of the four fingers gripping the brush, in certain circumstances, they are called upon to substitute for the wrist. This occurs when lines are drawn forward or backward between five and eleven o'clock or between six and twelve o'clock. For, in such cases, with the lower arm parallel to the tabletop, the range of mobility of the middle and fourth fingers in folding backward or forward at the wrist is not so badly restricted.

When the wrist is temporarily incapacitated, the fourth finger, supported by the little finger, must take over the function of the wrist in pushing the brush tuft forward or upward, while the middle finger works in the opposite direction by drawing it backward, balanced by its partner, the fourth finger. Such functions are important for effective brush tip control at the initial stage of each stroke.

However the effectiveness of such maneuvers is limited to the length of the brush handle and the height at which it is held by the fingers. Beyond that, the alternatives are: (1) to stand up to take full advantage of the arm and the shoulder; (2) to move the elbow forward and turn the hand sideways with the thumb pointing to the left; or (3) to shift the body sideways to achieve the same effect as described in (2).

Too many cooks spoil the broth

So far, we have briefly touched upon a number of functions discharged by parts of the human body including the fingers, the arm and elbow, etc. And, regardless of what has just been said about the ineffectiveness of the wrist in certain positions, in all other situations, it remains the most indispensable member of the setup.

Because of the unique character of the Chinese brush, vigor of linear expression and excellence in aesthetic delivery have always been the ideals of every exponent of Chinese painting. The disciplined execution of brushstrokes is inconceivable without the vigorous regulation of the wrist upon the various movements of the brush.

Consequently, to the beginner, early brushwork control is identifiable with one basic guideline: do not forget to hold all silent parts inoperative, or, if necessary, passively co-operative, whenever the wrist is on top of the action. Remember, "Too many cooks spoil the broth!"

Having said this we will now proceed to the next important subject of our study—the actual act of drawing a straight line with a loaded brush.
(A graphic illustration of the process of ink-loading, including double-loading for special effect, is given later.)

Drawing the spindle stroke with a loaded brush
Before setting the brush down to paint for the first time, it is beneficial to repeat one more time the pendulum test to get the feeling of the process involved before touching the paper with a loaded brush. Then check the shape of the tip and the amount of ink loaded in it and continue with the following preliminary exercises:

Spindle stroke test exercise
Test I
Begin by placing the upright brush about eight inches in front of you with the lower arm bent inward. Meanwhile the elbow remains on the table with the lower arm and the wrist slightly raised and free to move like the arm of a phonograph. Where it stops about eight inches from you, the tip of the brush would be directly over the spot which, for this exercise, will be marked as the center of the "pendulous" arc. Then, with the left hand (the free hand to the right-hander) steadying the wrist to prevent it from shifting out of position, rotate the wrist in a clockwise direction (W◡) so that the tip of the brush is now pointing to the left. Do not rotate more than 50° from the vertical, making use of the doorknob turning action described earlier.

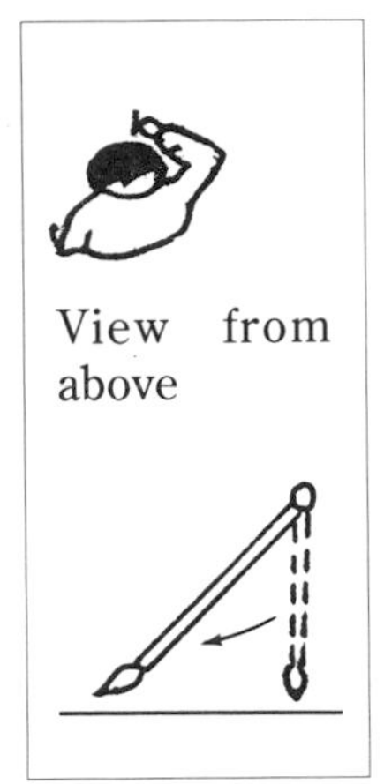

Test II.
From this position slowly drop the tip of the brush down on the paper and, as soon as contact is made, turn the wrist in the reverse direction to move the brush to the right (◡W). Since the tip is still pointing to the left, the bristles become somewhat compressed with the tip bent backward and trailing behind the handle, as shown here. As the handle approaches the center point, the bristles are compressed further, causing the line to widen until the brush moves past the vertical point at the center. Beyond this, the stroke tapers off to a sharp point at the end of the pendulous movement.

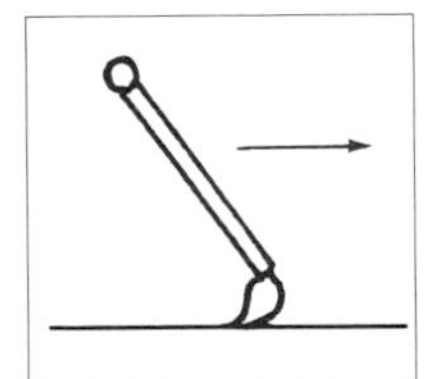

(Note that, as long as the wrist remains in a fixed position, the line produced would be restricted to a length of about one and half inches, unless a higher than normal hand hold is adopted.)

If the brush is steadfastly held in the upright position throughout the entire length of the stroke, the result would be a line in the shape of a spindle, as shown here. But if the figure does not bear any resemblance to a spindle, the cause may be attributed to one or more of the following problems:

Problem	Remedy
1. Ink flooding on contact	Tip overloaded. Remove excess liquid.
2. Head of spindle crooked	Tip not in proper shape. Roll it and smooth it over the side of the mixing dish (see "Rolling the Handle and Raised Hand").
3. The line wavers	The wrist shifts out of position, thereby nullifying the straight-forwardness of a pendulous movement.
4. A blunted head at the beginning	The tip is set down at an angle not slanted correctly. Thus the sharp butt of the tip does not show up in full.
5. A short aborted end zone	Stroke begun too far to the left of the center point of the line (see Step II of section on the pendulum stroke).
6. Main body not wide enough or, conversely, too wide	Either adjust the height of your grip on the handle or the height of your wrist to raise the brush.
7. Tapering effect not well-proportioned	Check the posture of the handle to make sure it is held in the vertical, upright position from beginning to end.

Most common flaws are the result of (1) the head, (2) the main body and (3) the tail end not being properly rendered. In most cases, the tip alone is concerned either in (1) or (3) and the belly hairs in (2).

The dual character of the upright brush
The list of malformed strokes shows that failure to correctly apply the "upright brush" technique is at the root of most problems faced by a beginner. However, although the term "upright brush" is frequently cited in publications dealing with painting and calligraphy, what constitutes such a mode of brushwork in terms of the technical skills involved has never been clearly defined.

On the other hand, drawing the brush in the vertical position generally results in the tip being positioned at the center of the stroke; which means that, from that point of view, the "upright brush" may well be just another name for the calligraphic technique known as the "center tip" brush.

Meanwhile, to add to the confusion, under certain circumstances the slanted brush can also be operated with the tip held at the center of the stroke, as shown here.

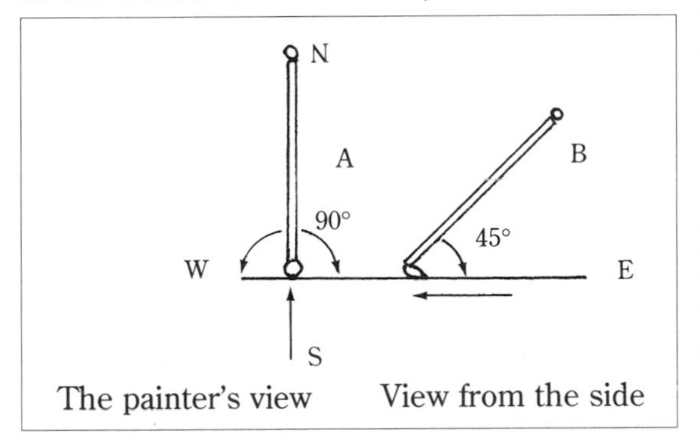

The painter's view View from the side

Whether the handle of a brush is perceived to be in the upright or slanted mode depends entirely on the particular perspective of the viewer in question.

In the chapter on the Bamboo, the first Paragon, the reader will have ample opportunities to practice the type of brushwork known by either the one or the other of the above terms.

The need to roll and twist the brush hairs
The tip of the brush is made of a few of the longest hairs. By comparison with the other parts of the brush, it is the softest and the weakest; and yet it is constantly in action. It is the most important part of the assembly, if only because so much of the work load is placed on so few hairs.

Since the tip is always the first to make contact with the paper, it is responsible for making the right move at the very beginning of a stroke. To ensure that the beginning is neat and firm, pressure is seldom applied on the tip at the point of impact.

Variation in the width of a painted line is of aesthetic significance in Chinese brushwork; thus, contact is usually initiated with the tip in the slanted mode. This will allow for gradual expansion of width as the stroke takes shape. (Exception to the rule: when it is pointed straight down to produce a dot or an extremely thin line.)

To secure effective control of the few tip hairs upon contact, the tip should be twisted in a moderate "roll" as it begins to move in the desired direction. As with a piece of string, twisting the soft fibers turns them into a stiff and manageable strand which will yet remain sufficiently pliable to be responsive to manipulation.

This is the reason why most brushstrokes in Chinese calligraphy or painting begin with the tip pointing at a tangent off the intended course before the wrist takes over in a ⤹W or W⤸ turn as the case may be, to bring it in line along the designated course. (Exception to the rule: the tip would face exactly in the opposite direction, i.e. bent backward, if the stroke has the shape of a spindle such as the Sunshine Bamboo Leaf in the next chapter.)

The ice-skating troupers syndrome

This occurs when the tip and the belly move at disparate speed.

When the brush is rolled in the slanted position for turning and strengthening the tip hairs, the tip and the belly will move at different speeds, as shown in the diagram below depicting two stroke movements, with T-1 and B-1 forming the first move and T-2 and B-2 the second one.

Such split acceleration turns are required when there is a change in the width of the line simultaneously with a change of direction from the starting position. (See head section of bamboo stem in chapter on Bamboo.) As in the case of the bamboo stem, there is a momentary pause on the downstroke as the belly hair leads the move with a 45° turn to the right—for the right-handed person—during which it has to move faster to cover a longer distance by comparison with the tip. Once the turn is

Opening action (preliminary)
(Tip only moving up from upright position)

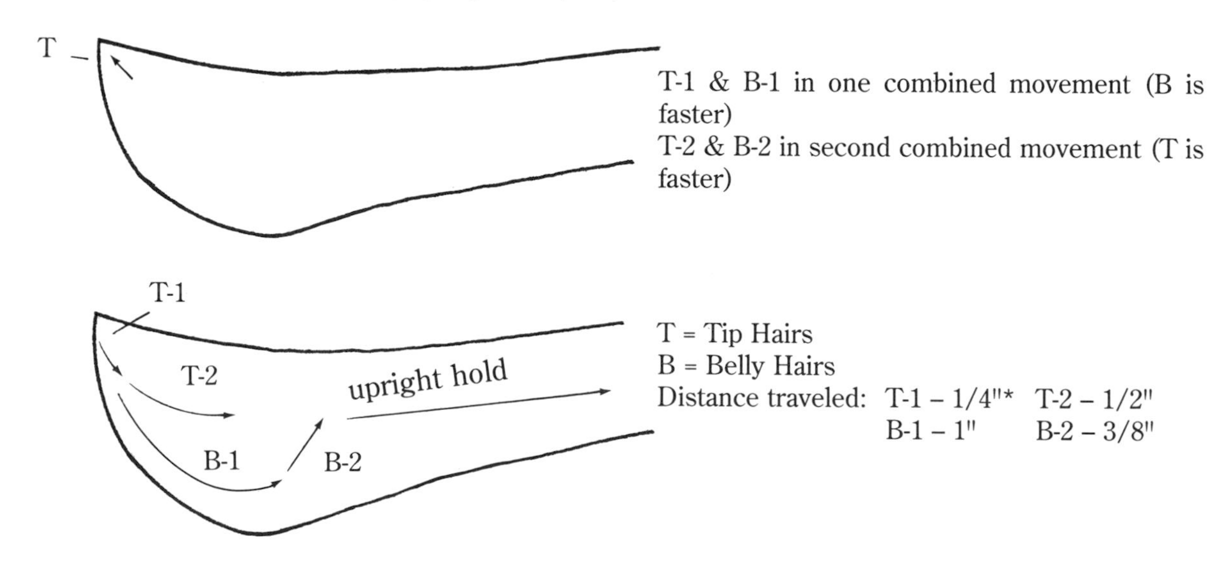

* Above figure is magnified. For smaller sizes, maximum T-1 distance is 1/8".

completed, the situation is reversed with the tip scrambling to move alongside the belly before the stroke enters into the straight, narrow section in the middle of the stem.

Actually what happens here is analogous to what ice-skaters in a dance troupe do when they have to make an about-face, holding hands in a straight line, in which the anchor dancer makes only a standing turn while the skater at the opposite end has to scamper at top speed to keep up with the rest of the group. Beginners not familiar with the workings of Chinese brushwork should keep in mind the typical maneuvers of the ice-skaters when they study the bamboo stem for the first time. Failure to hold the tip in position during the first part of the movement would result in the formation of a pair of steer horns.

The brush as a ballerina
A parallel feature of the technique of "rolling the tip" in split acceleration turns is the attendant up-and-down movement of the brush needed when momentary pressure is applied upon the tip hairs in the course of such turns. Such pressure is essential for effective control of the tip working in a compressed, twisted state; the effect is indeed similar to the pulsating movements that ballerinas make with their feet as they pirouette on their toes, a movement which is not only graceful, but also physically and aesthetically an integral element of ballet dancing. (There is one exception though: pressure is never applied on the brush standing vertically on its tip the way the ballerina does on her toes.)

USEFUL POINTS TO REMEMBER
The following is a summary of useful points of general interest:

- *The separate functions of the fingers and the wrist*

The fingers are to grip the handle of the brush firmly, yet not too vigorously as to cause the hand to cramp if kept at it too long. And it pays to keep in mind that, as the primary conveyance of motive power from the forearm, the wrist is the principal steersman of most types of brushwork in general.

- *The need for graduated pressure as applied to the brush hair*

Pressure is not supposed to be exerted upon the brush at a fixed, uniform intensity at all times. There are many occasions when the maximum force required is nothing more than letting the hand sink into the brush, much in the same way as the technique termed *dun* (lowering or bowing) in Chinese calligraphy. More about the need for fine-tuning the process will be detailed in the section dealing with the slanted brush.

- *The role of the arm in changing stroke direction*

Like the pendulum cited earlier, the wrist in performing the "doorknob" or "key-turning" action is feasible only in one direction. Consequently, changing direction in the middle of a stroke would require the arm to be simultaneously shifted to a new position based on the previous profile relative to the bottom line of the paper.

- *A way to check the veracity of the upright brush*

In the execution of brushstrokes of a very fine and deliberate character, the vertical brush is all-important. One way to ensure that the hand is doing its part correctly is to see to it that the ends of the two bones of the forearm—the radius and ulna—are held level with the tabletop as closely as possible. (At the start of the vertical stroke, the radius is on a slightly higher level than the ulna, but will drop down in a C roll as the wrist makes the CW turn.) Of these two bones, the radius is the larger one from which the wrist draws its power to carry out the CW turn. Thus, it is the important one to watch. Unaccustomed to this posture of the hand, the novice may feel a certain amount of tension around the wrist at first. But once the skill is mastered, the effect is remarkable.

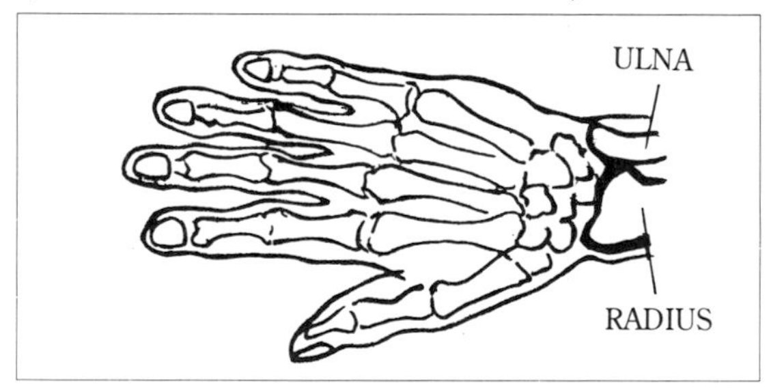

- *The three modes of the slanted brush*

Two different forms of the slanted brush technique are known in Chinese calligraphy: the "sidelong mode" and the "flat mode." However, the terms are of little assistance to the uninitiated if he is not explained the precise manipulative differences between the two modes in actual practice. Earlier we have noted that the reservoir of the ink is formed in the upper half of the tuft of a brush. This means that, at the most, only about half the length of the bristles is used for painting. If we divide this working area into three separate zones graded from 1 to 3, the result will be roughly as shown on the next page:

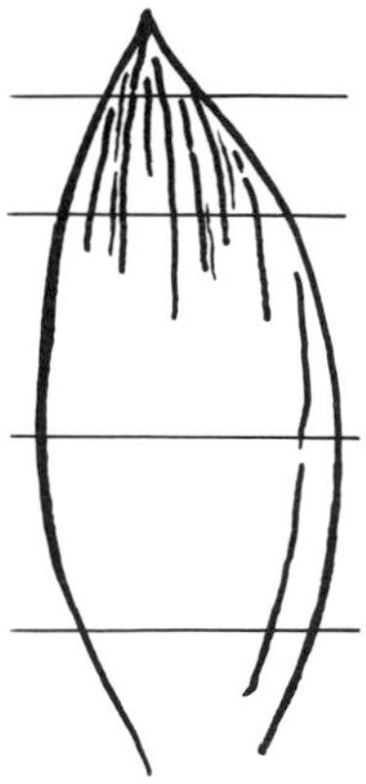

Shape of Tuft		Zone Area	Symbol	Call Word	Type of Stroke
1		0 – .5	TP	Tip	Extremely fine line
2		.5 – 1	BH or ST	Belly Hair/Sit	Most young branches
3		1 – 2	BH-1	Belly-one	Larger branches, pressure applied
4	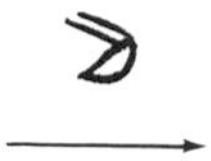	2 – 3	BH-2	Belly-two	Bamboo stalks, etc., maximum pressure applied

The above represents a simplified spectrum of the effect produced at various stages of the slanted brush. Nevertheless, in the classroom, the system has been found to work well in joint exercises where the teacher uses only the call words to describe the brushwork involved in drawing a simple sunshine bamboo leaf.

Key to Symbols Used

RS	Ready station
⌂	Upright hold with slanted hold shown as ⌂
🡅 or ↑	Direction of stroke
▽	Brush tip in preparatory position before impact
△-(11)	Brush tip pointing at 11 o'clock
△-(11) 🡅	Brush tip pointing at 11 o'clock but stroke movement is directed toward 2 o'clock
W◡)	The wrist rolling as when it is turning a key in the clockwise direction
(◡W	The wrist rotating in the anti-clockwise direction
Wr	Wrist action area
T	Tip of brush
TH	Tip hair
BH	Belly hair
BH-1	Part of hair measured from the tip up including BH-2, etc.
ϕ	Brush tip held to the center of the stroke
P	Pressure point (P↓ indicates application of pressure, and P↑, release of pressure)
ST	To lower brush without pressure, equivalent to "crouching" in calligraphy
LF	Lifting, or lifting off from surface area
Ar	Arm action area
LA	Lower arm action; may also involve whole arm participation depending on direction and length of stroke in question
⟨e⟩	Elbow to remain in stationary position
Ⓔ	Elbow released from stationary position
CP or ⊙	Indicates center point, which may also be represented by a dot or a cross + or ⊕ where brush movement is not involved
X	Momentary pause (or a slash as in BH/ST, indicating a momentary break between two separate actions)
S	Slowly
SL	Slower
GO	Move briskly

DK	Dark area (or shaded area)
∽	S-turn
R.S.B.	Top of the brush handle pointing approximately at the person's right shoulder blade
Ad.A	Top of handle pointing approximately at the Adam's apple

THE BAMBOO

Bamboos are found in most temperate regions of China, south of the Yang Zi River. During the Northern Song dynasty (960–1121) the bamboo became a favorite subject for professional artists as well as scholar-poets. As accomplished calligraphers, they were the first ones to explore the close affinity between the art of monochrome ink painting of this plant and the technique of calligraphic brush treatment. To the common folk, the exalting nobility of this graceful plant, its flexible, yielding pliability and its ability to bend and move with the storms symbolize the lofty attributes of a perfect gentleman—the first of the Paragons to be examined in detail in this book.

As Chinese brush painting is essentially a linear art, studying the bamboo first is most appropriate because it consists of mainly straight line strokes and very little else. Nevertheless, as the student learns about the frequent changes in light and heavy color tones of individual parts of the plant in a painting, he soon becomes aware of the classic principle of the unity of dissimilar elements observed in Oriental artwork, popularly alluded to as the *Yin* and *Yang* of the *Dao* (*Tao*) of Chinese painting.

From Spindle Stroke to Bamboo Leaf (Type 1)

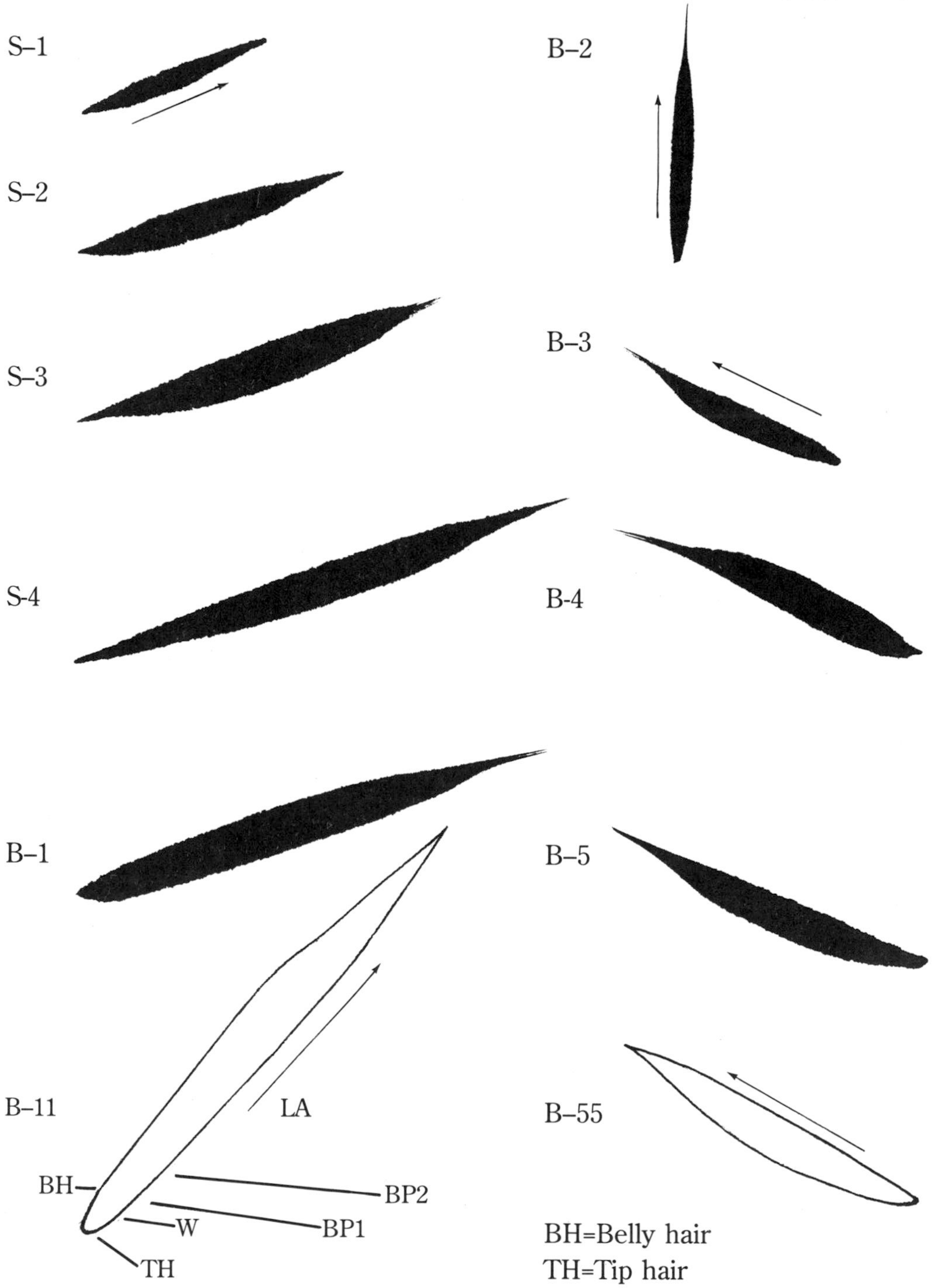

S–1

B–2

S–2

B–3

S–3

S-4

B-4

B–1

B–5

B–11

LA

BH

BP2

W

BP1

TH

B–55

BH=Belly hair
TH=Tip hair

Strokes S-1 to S-4 should be taken up before the B series representing up-pointing bamboo leaves. With B-1, they are placed on the left side of the page which renders them more difficult to execute as the wrist of a right-hander would not be able to operate an upstroke from the left margin. Therefore, at first, the paper should be moved to the right and gradually moved back to the original position until the mechanics of the stroke become familiar. In reality this stroke can often occur where it is not conveniently located closer to the right hand.

On the upstroke B-2, the same pendulous action is used except that the elbow is extended to allow the wrist to operate with the lower arm almost parallel to the bottom line of the paper. If the subject is located higher up on the paper, a slight forward and right shift of the body may be necessary.

On the other hand, the normal doorknob action is not feasible with strokes moving up toward 10 o'clock such as figures B-3 to B-5. In these examples, the elbow has to be raised to the level of the wrist off the table and, at the approach of the final lift-off of the tip, to move along with the entire hand in a continuous downward-upward curved movement to lift the tip up and away from the paper in a straight line.

The same hindrance applies to B-3 etc., when they are located at the lower right-hand side of the paper. The student will find that they are easier to draw if placed higher up on the left side.

The sharp opening head of a "spindle" stroke can be more rounded if there is a momentary pause at the white area of the diagram shown here. This allows the ink at the tip to spread out freely to form a smooth and well-shaped head of the bamboo leaf, provided that the brush is not overloaded. Check the shape of the tip before applying this technique to begin such a stroke.

Details of outlined figure B-11

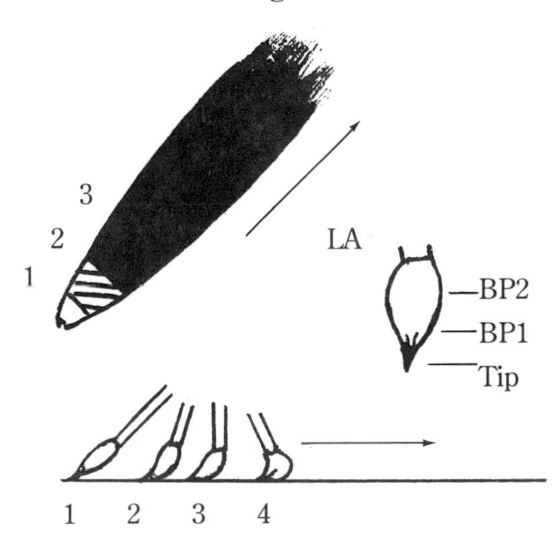

1. White area = Tip of brush
2. Shaded area = BP1 = Belly-one
3. Black area = BP2 = Belly-two

LA = Lower arm in action.

Action details:
1. Tip lowered to make contact.
2. Wrist begins doorknob turn CW.
3. Increased pressure as handle approaches 90° vertical point. From here on the wrist directs the forward motion.
4. Handle passed center point; noticeable decrease in pressure. Now move forward resolutely.
5. Where action develops beyond the operational range of the wrist, the lower arm too has to move forward as sustained pressure is applied all the way until the tip is lifted at the end of the stroke.

Details of Brushwork on Sunshine Bamboo Leaves

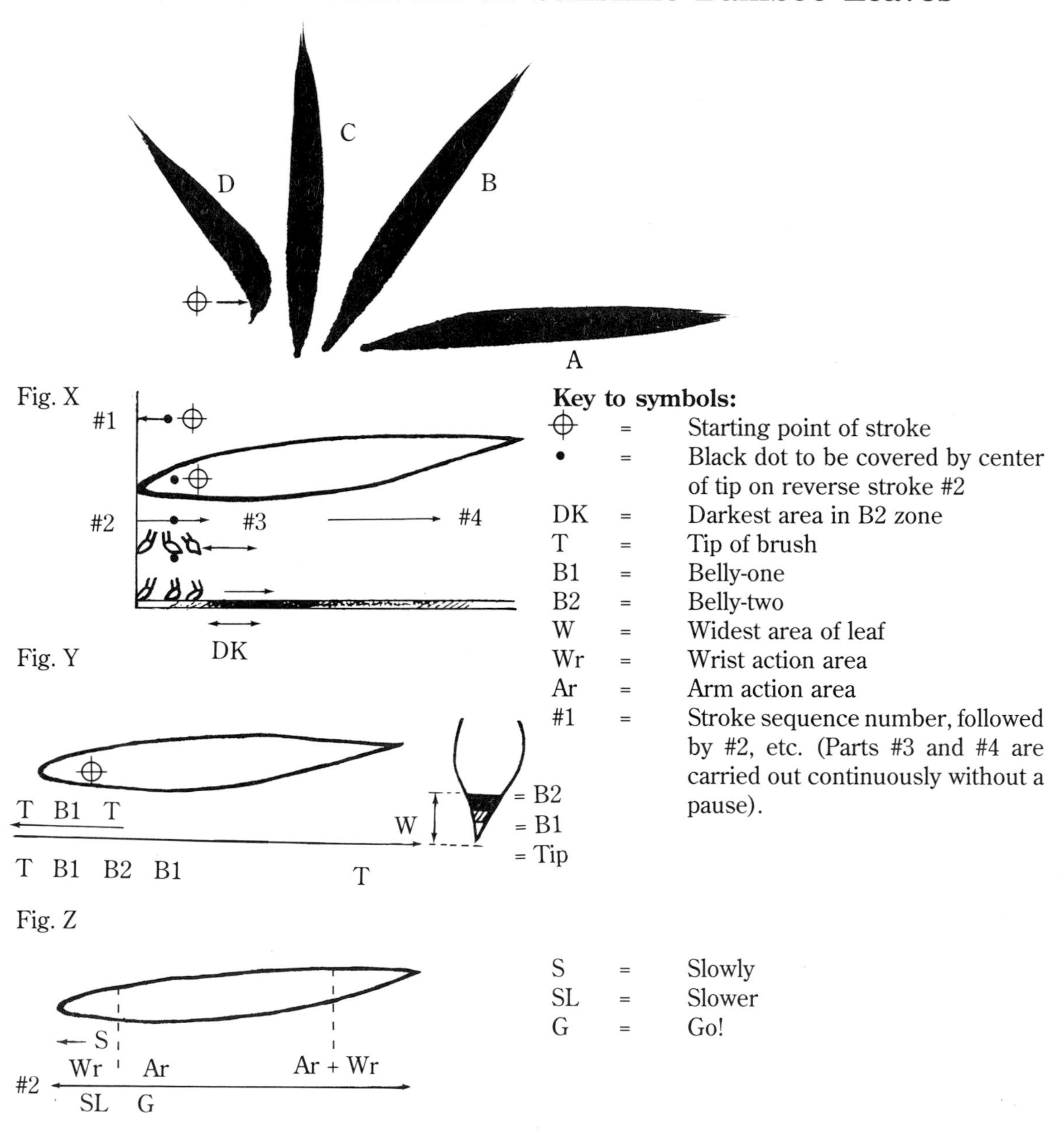

The directions apply to all examples except for D on the far left. In D, #1 moves down toward 6 o'clock and, as the brush reverses direction in #2, the wrist makes a CW turn near ⊕ before B2 ushers in the straight sector between #3 and #4. The elbow is raised up to assist in lifting the brush off the paper at the end of the stroke.

Additional brushwork details on sunshine bamboo leaves

Diagrams X, Y and Z on the preceding page illustrate brushwork on sunshine leaves viewed from three different perspectives.

In the upper half of Figure X, you are looking down at the outlined contour of a bamboo leaf from the perspective of a person bending over it with brush in hand in normal working posture. Underneath the outlined figure of a leaf are side views of different postures of the tufts of brushes as they appear in their respective positions along two tracks indicated by the arrows #1 and #2 off to one side of the head of the leaf.

At the bottom of Figure X is a second track with shaded areas representing the degrees of intensity of pressure applied on the brush along the path of the brushstroke between points #3 and #4. Here the shaded area represents medium pressure (B1); the dark area, increased pressure (B2); and the blank area, minimum pressure (T). The letters DK under the short length of the dark area emphasize the fact that heavy pressure lasts only a very brief moment and is reduced forthwith to the B1 level all the way through until shortly before the end of the stroke.

Figure Y reflects the relation between the amount of pressure applied and the corresponding width of the stroke represented by the letter "W" next to the figure of a brush tuft shown in the vertical position.

Figure Z on the other hand shows the changing speed of the stroke from the beginning to the end and the part of the wrist or arm involved through three different zones.

Two- or Three-Leaf Group Formation with Supporting Twigs

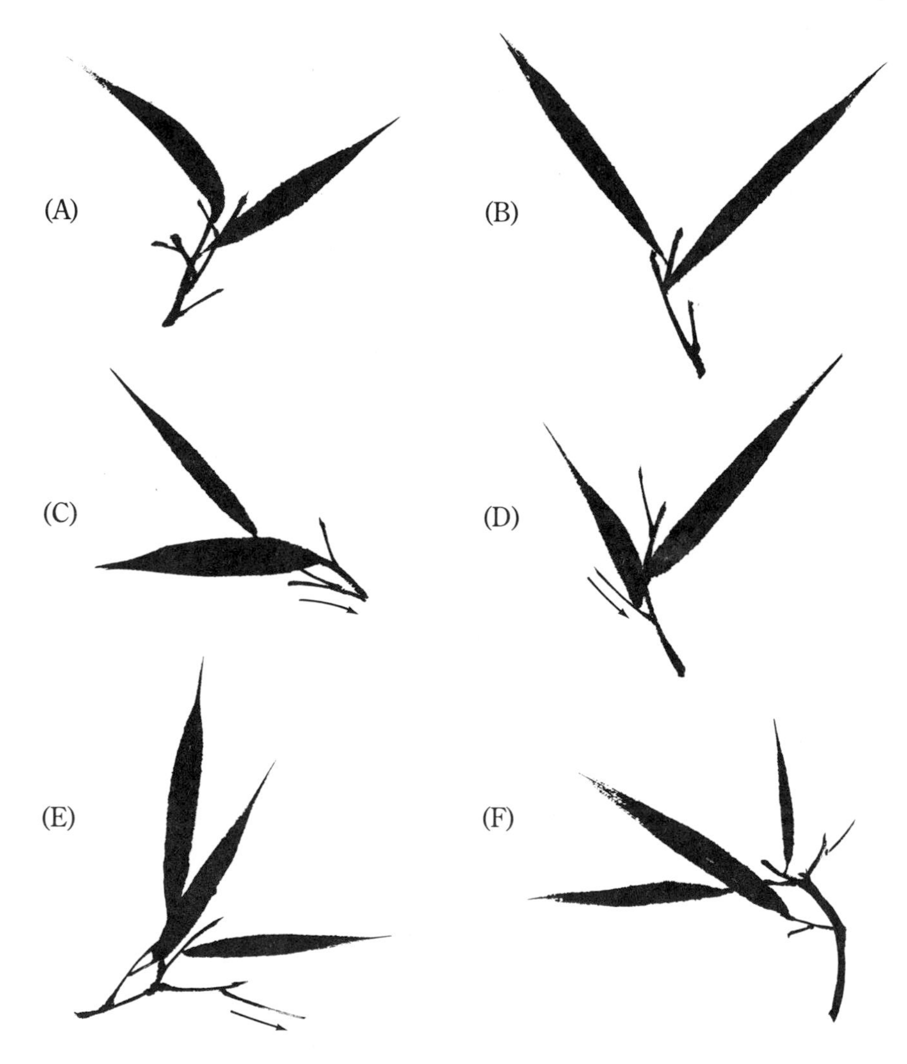

1. All strokes on the leaves move from the base toward the tip.
2. Practice in the order indicated by the letters (A), (B), etc. In each group, start with the leaf moving from left to right. In practice, however, the choice is optional.
3. All strokes on the branches or twigs move away from the person, except those marked with an arrow as in (C), (D) and (E) where the lines extend from the top left down toward the lower right side of the paper, which involve the kind of action described as "against the grain" strokes in "Pendulum In Your Hand."

Sunshine Bamboo

Example SB-1

Sunshine Bamboo

Example SB-2

An Elementary Composition

Planning a Simple Composition

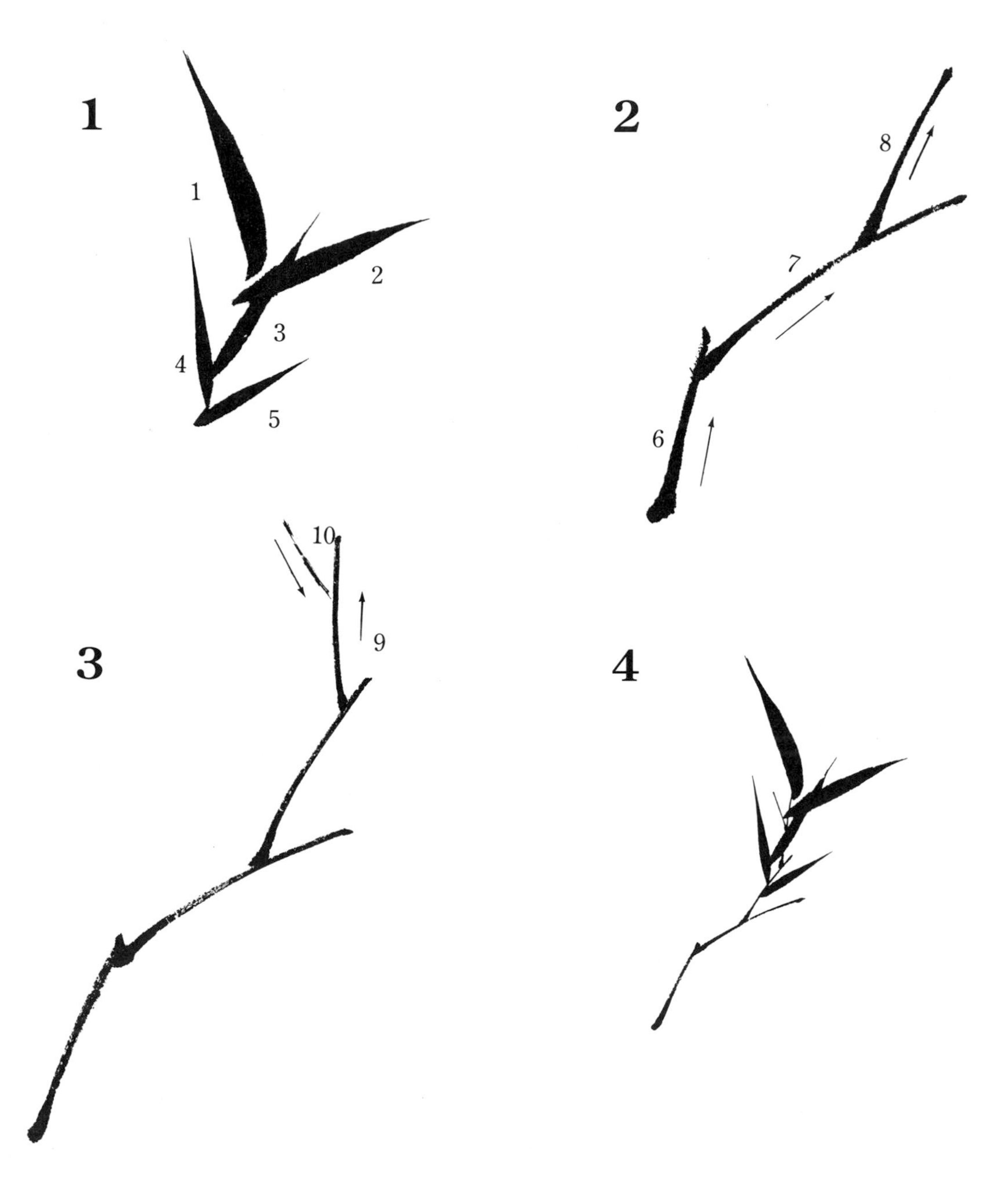

On a simple composition of only a few leaves, set the leaves down first and then paint the branches as shown.

The Bamboo Tree with the Up-waving Sunshine Leaves

This type of bamboo is known under various names in Chinese manuals, from "Upward-tilted Bamboo" to "Fine-weather Bamboo." Here it is called the "Up-waving Sunshine Bamboo" which is more descriptive of its youthful character.

The process of double-loading the ink mixture

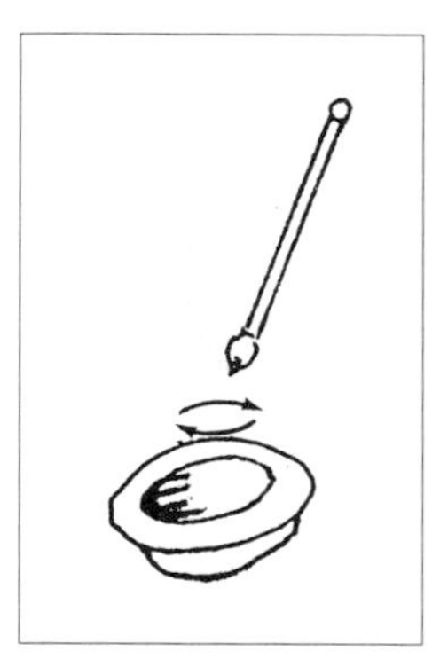

1. Prepare medium gray mixture. Stir thoroughly and set aside in one section of mixing dish. Then test color of mixture on a piece of absorbent paper. If necessary, add ink or water until desired shade is obtained. Stir again to ensure even distribution.

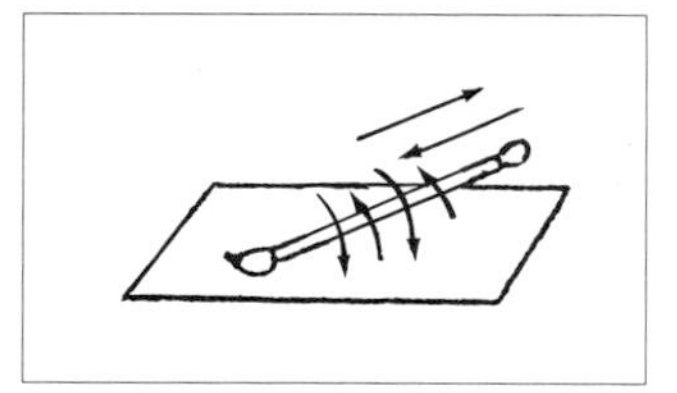

2. Rinse brush in clean water. Then wipe the tuft over a piece of absorbent paper to remove excess water. Roll the handle as illustrated here.

3. Dip the brush in medium gray mixture* up to 3/4 of the length of the tuft. Stir the mixture to ensure uniform color tone intake. Scrape the front of the brush lightly over the side of the mixing dish to remove excess moisture and prepare the tip for the second loading process.

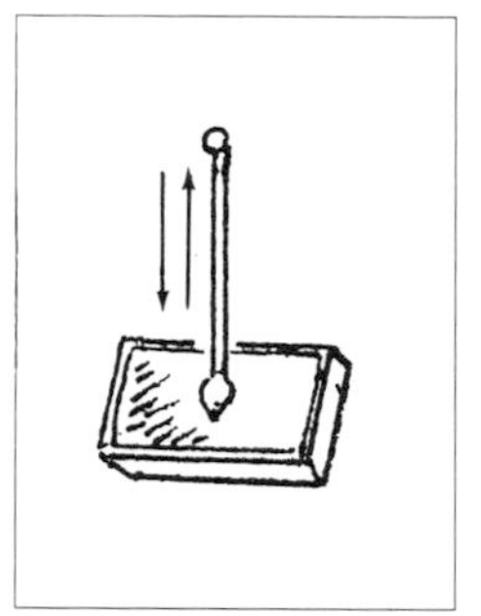

4. Holding the brush upright, carefully dip the tip straight down to pick up undiluted ink to the depth of about 1/8" measured from the tip. Then, with one light dab on a piece of paper, check for correct division of dark and light color zones at the tip. If necessary, return to (2) and start again.

5. Check the shape of the tip after loading. If it does not show a sharp pointed end (as when it is new), it is probably overloaded; in which case scrape again on a piece of absorbent paper, but involving only the part that is out of shape.

Important note:
In checking for correct two-tone color division as explained in (4), the brush should be held at an oblique angle but only low enough to affect the portion around the tip so as not to reach the mixture contained higher up in the area of the belly.

You should make it a point to check the shape of the tip as detailed in (5) each time before you set down the brush to start painting. With few exceptions, the tip should be straight and in good shape before use.

For one-color loading, omit the second part of (3) and the entire (4).

* If the main body of the stem is a very light color, then even clear water may be used. This type of double-loading is not as easy as the kind carried out with the background-wash brush detailed in Type 2. However, by using the ordinary painting brush, it is possible to do stems of varying widths without changing brushes.

The Sections of A Bamboo Stem

Like the sugar cane, the bamboo grows in sections of varying lengths separated by a prominent ridge at the junctions. Thus, while each section is basically straight and of uniform width, the ends are wider where they join another section.

Since the stem can grow up to several inches in diameter, the slanted brush is used to take full advantage of the belly hairs in drawing a stem of the size illustrated in the next section.

For obvious reasons, the "pendulum" principle of the upright brush recommended for drawing the leaves would not work here. Rather than a simple straight line, here we are concerned with three formative changes in the contours of both ends of each section of the bamboo stem: (1) a convex curvature at the beginning followed by (2) a gradual slimming down of the line and (3) ending in a long, straight midsection of uniform width. The same modification, except (3), is repeated at the end of each section.

The illustration below shows in detail the principal steps in the process of drawing the head part of a section up to the straight midsection of uniform width.

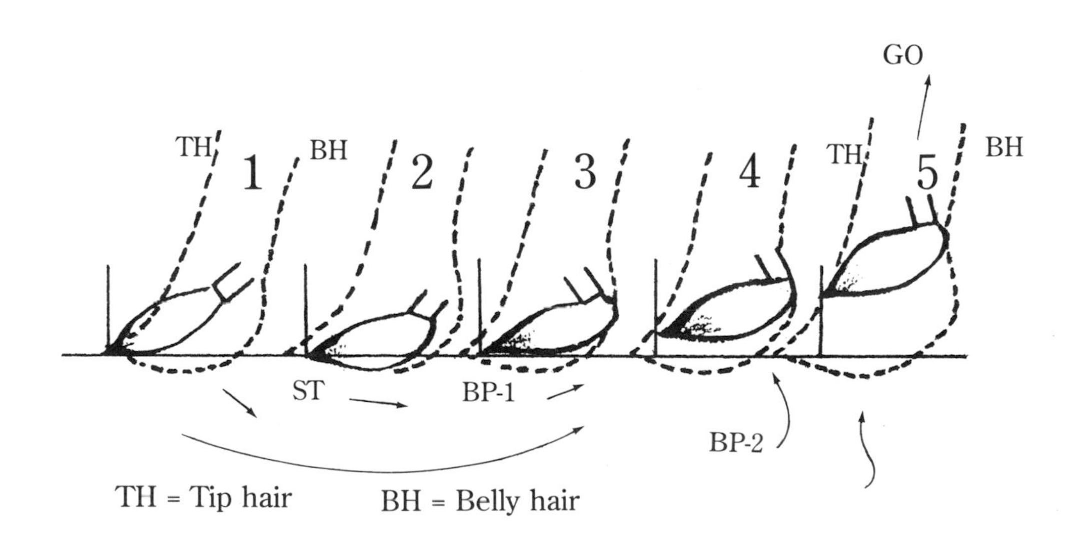

Step 1

Immediately as the brush is set down, it is drawn backward at an angle indicated by the arrow under figure 1.

Step 2

In proceeding from Step 1 to Step 2, pressure is applied on the belly hairs while the handle and the tuft are dropped to a lower level.

Step 3

A determined doorknob turn of the wrist—(↺W BP-2*P)—pushes the base of the belly upward. This broadens the width of the line in that area. Note that, up to this point, the tip has moved only a short distance (see vertical line markers) with the wrist directing all the movements as necessary.

Step 4

The sharp turn from 3 to 4 is accomplished with the co-ordinated support of the whole arm: (1) the stroke reaches the point where the wrist has reached the normal limit of continuing to turn to the right; and (2) the necessity of shifting the brush to a higher level and of slimming down the width of the line at the same time. (See arrow under fig. 4.)

Step 5

A second change of direction occurs at this point where the belly has to draw a moderate S-turn (indicated by the arrow under figure 5). Meanwhile the top of the handle is raised and lowered again as the brush begins to move resolutely along the straight midsection with the palm of the hand turned outward more or less in the direction of the tip.

In terms of the rhythm of the entire operation, the first three steps may be taken together as a continuous movement conducted by the wrist as indicated by the larger arrow extending from figure 1 to figure 3. Speed is reduced slightly only as pressure is increased at Step 3.

The symbols TH and BH clearly show that, from Step 3 onward, the belly hairs lead the way with the tip trailing behind so that the darker ink mixture in the tip is kept at a distance from the side displaying a lighter color tone.

An example of two complete sections joined together is given in the section "The First Section of a Bamboo Stem."

* For explanation of 'BP-2', see "From Spindle Stroke to Bamboo Leaf."

Practicing The First Part of A Bamboo Section in Four Separate Steps*

A

Practice only the belly turn and try to move the tip as little as possible.

B

After the belly turn, raise the handle and steer the brush toward a more horizontal plane.

C

Now repeat step B but start to pull the tip down while the belly is slowing down in B-2. The tip line shown on the left is protruding due to handle not raised to proper height.

D

Correct shape appears as tip line is deliberately pulled down in a moderate curvature and the brush is simultaneously raised to the upright position in a co-ordinated action.

> *In the beginning there was no method, but method came into being based on one stroke, for the single stroke is the root of all representation.*
>
> Shi Tao—*Hua Yu Lu*

*See Diagram X, "Ice-skating Troupers Syndrome," in the Introduction.

Bamboo Branches and Stroke Directions for Left- or Right-Handed Persons

With few exceptions, the brushwork for bamboo branches is the same as detailed earlier for the stalks. Besides being more supple than the heavier stalks, the slender size of the young branches presupposes a more simplified brushwork:

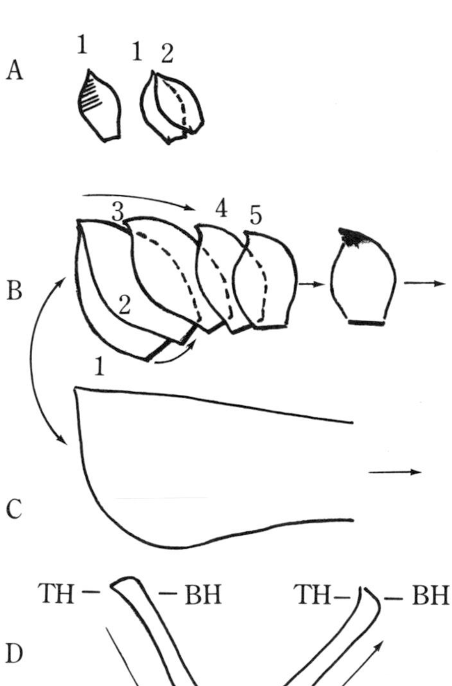

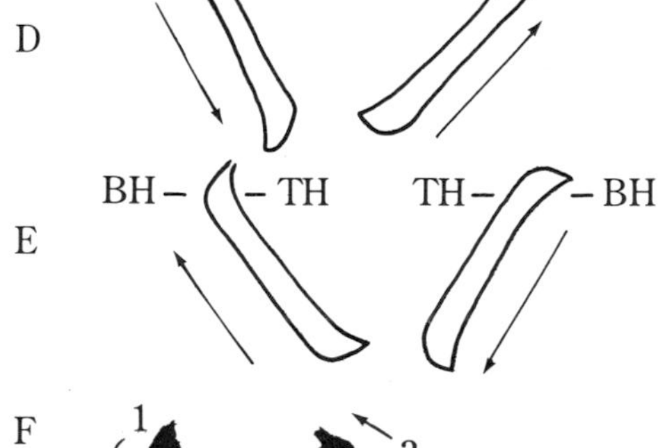

A 1. First lean on the belly hair on the left side (shaded area of Fig.1).
2. With the tip in a fixed position, press on the belly hair while shifting it upward in a CW action (see small arrow under 1 and 2 in B).

B3/4. So far the brush is slanted. The tip starts to move to the right as the brush is raised to a higher level and the line begins to slim down.
5. Tip and belly now move together with the brush held in the upright position as the stroke enters upon the straight sector of the stroke.

C The contour formed by the brushwork detailed in A and B inclusive.

D Directions for right-handed persons. TH = Tip Hair; BH = Belly Hair.

E Directions for left-handed persons.

F The directions on the ridge marks are for right-handed persons. Left-handers should reverse the shape of the figures and work in the opposite directions. All strokes marked 1 and 3 are slanted. Those shown as 2 are best carried out with the brush held upright and executed with the necessary action of the wrist.

Exercises for Bamboo Branches and Medium Size Trunks

Beginning Downstroke
Details of # 5

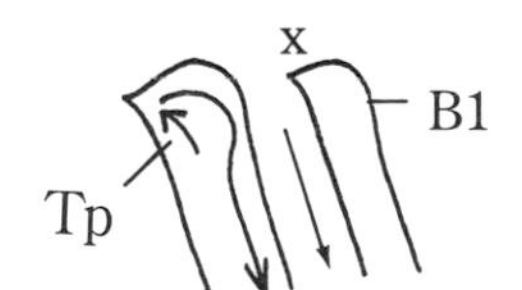

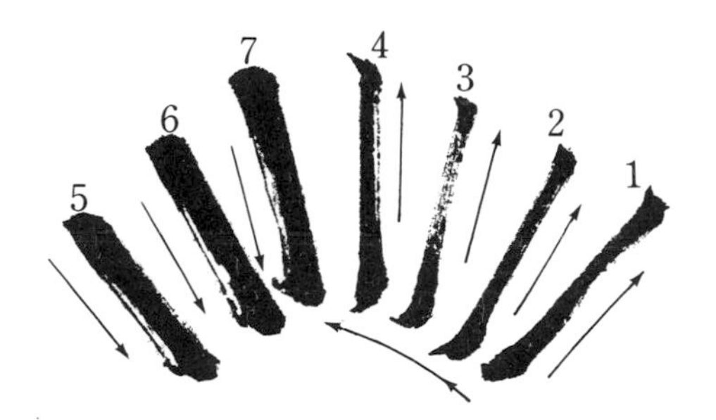

End of Upstroke
Details of # 1

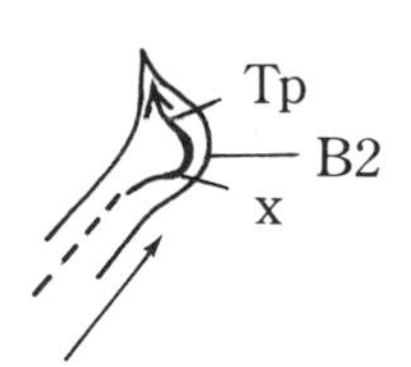

For right-handers:
Move elbow forward progressively from 1 to 7

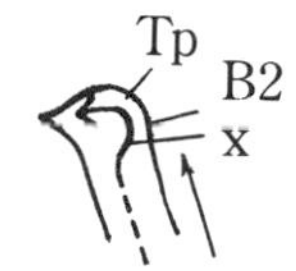

Examples for left-handers

#5 transposed to Upstroke   #1 becomes Downstroke

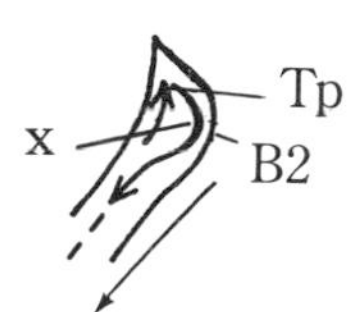

Tp = Tip
B1 = Belly-one
x = Momentary pause

End zone brushwork for E

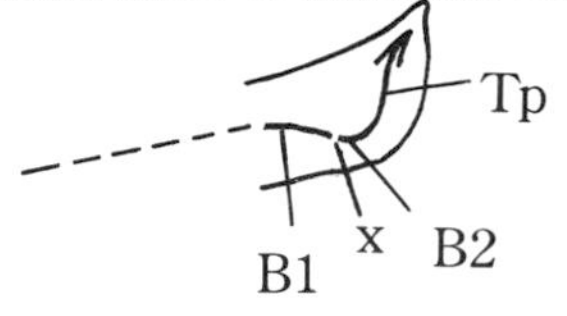

On branches and twigs it is important to work with a drier brush held upright.

The examples above are for the study of the head section of the branches. Example E terminates with an ending to be connected with another section behind it. (By reversing the directions in the end zone for E, left-handers can use the diagram to start a branch moving in the opposite direction. The reversed end zone for right-handers is then turned into a head section pointing the other way.)

A to E and 1 to 7 represent the order in which to study the examples.

The First Sections of A Bamboo Stem

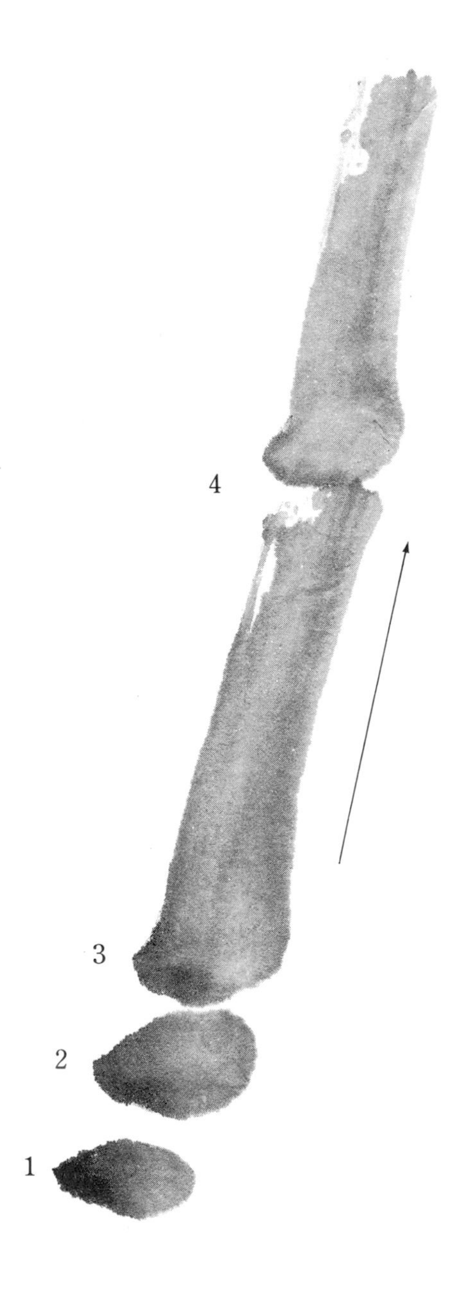

Additional Notes of General Interest

The figures illustrated here and on the following page are drawn with a double-loaded brush. Characteristic of the slanted brush employed here, the tip of the brush is confined to the left-hand side throughout the length of the stroke. This can be seen in the darker shade on one side of the bamboo stems, notably in the first few sections.

The first section (steps 1 to 4 inclusive) represents the lowest one above ground. The same procedures are applicable to additional sections higher up, but with one exception: the length of each succeeding section expands as the tree grows taller. However, the trend is reversed near the top of the tree.

If two or more stems are shown standing side-by-side, it is advisable to stagger their sections to different levels so the sectional "ridge" marks would not be seen right next to each other. This is to avoid a stiff arrangement.

Where more than three stems are arranged in a row, application of different color tones on each would set them apart to highlight the effect of three-dimensional presentation.

The steps shown here are for drawing bamboo stems with upstrokes. It is also possible to depict them with downstrokes, a reversed mode of brushwork which will be addressed later.

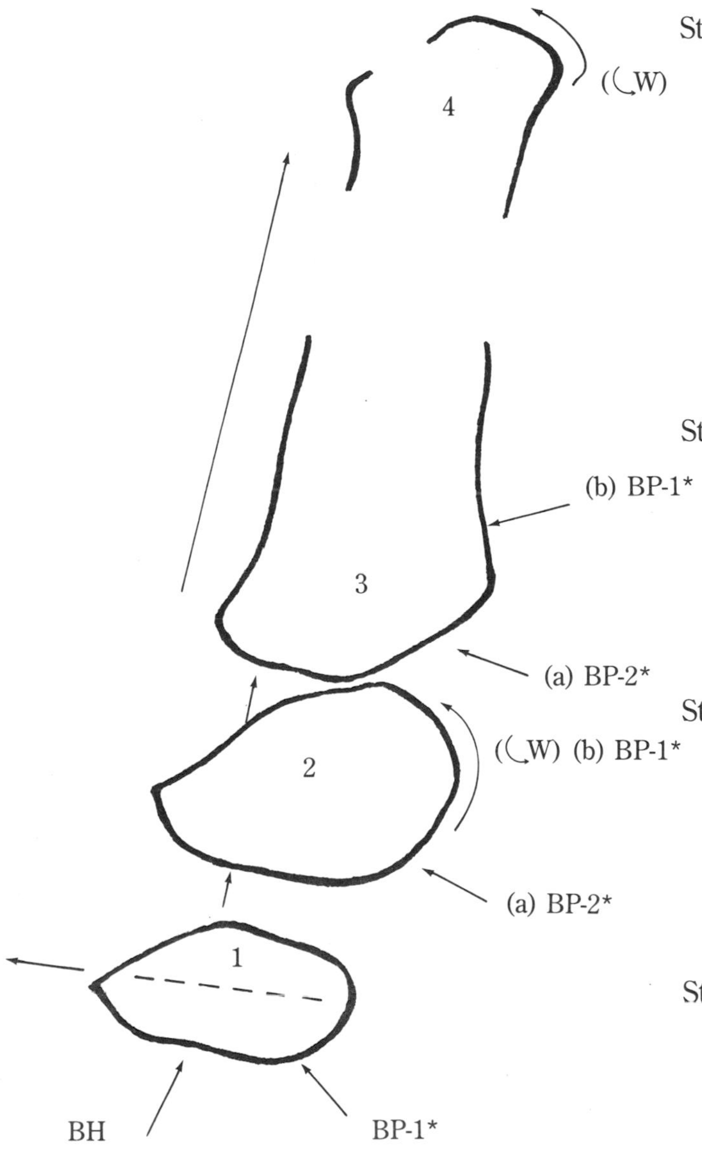

Step 4

The stroke slows down as the wrist is dropped to a lower level. In so doing it goes through another ↺W turn simultaneously widening the width of the line before the brush is lifted off the paper in the general direction of 10 o'clock (indicated by the arrow in the outlined figure 4 on the left).

Step 3

The wrist reaches its highest level at (b). Holding steadfastly the same height and posture at that point, it begins to push the brush forward, assisted by the whole arm.

Step 2

Rotate the wrist anti-clockwise (↺W). Pressure is briefly stepped up and gradually released as the brush is raised to a higher level until the wrist reaches the end of its turn at (b) BP-1* (Step 3).

Step 1

Set the brush down with its tip pointing to the left at an angle of about 20° (see arrow aligned with dotted lines). Initial pressure is applied at BP-1.

* See "From Spindle Stroke to Bamboo Leaf."

Bamboo Stems in Different Shades and Sizes

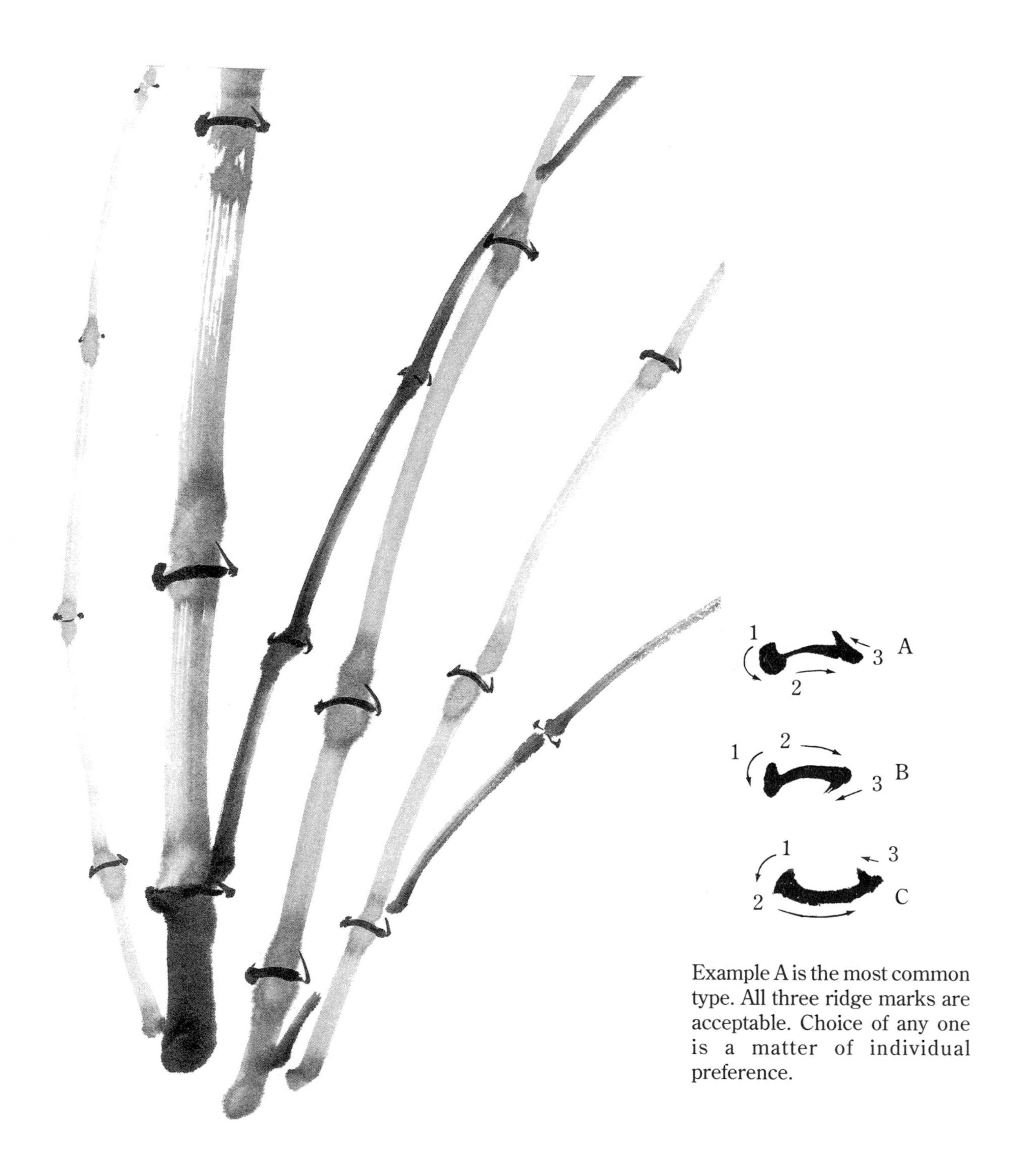

Example A is the most common type. All three ridge marks are acceptable. Choice of any one is a matter of individual preference.

The Sunshine Bamboo (Type 1)

The Sunshine Bamboo (Type 1)

Unlike the previous elementary composition, the stem and the primary branches are put in place first before the leaves. The smallest shoots are added at random at the end.

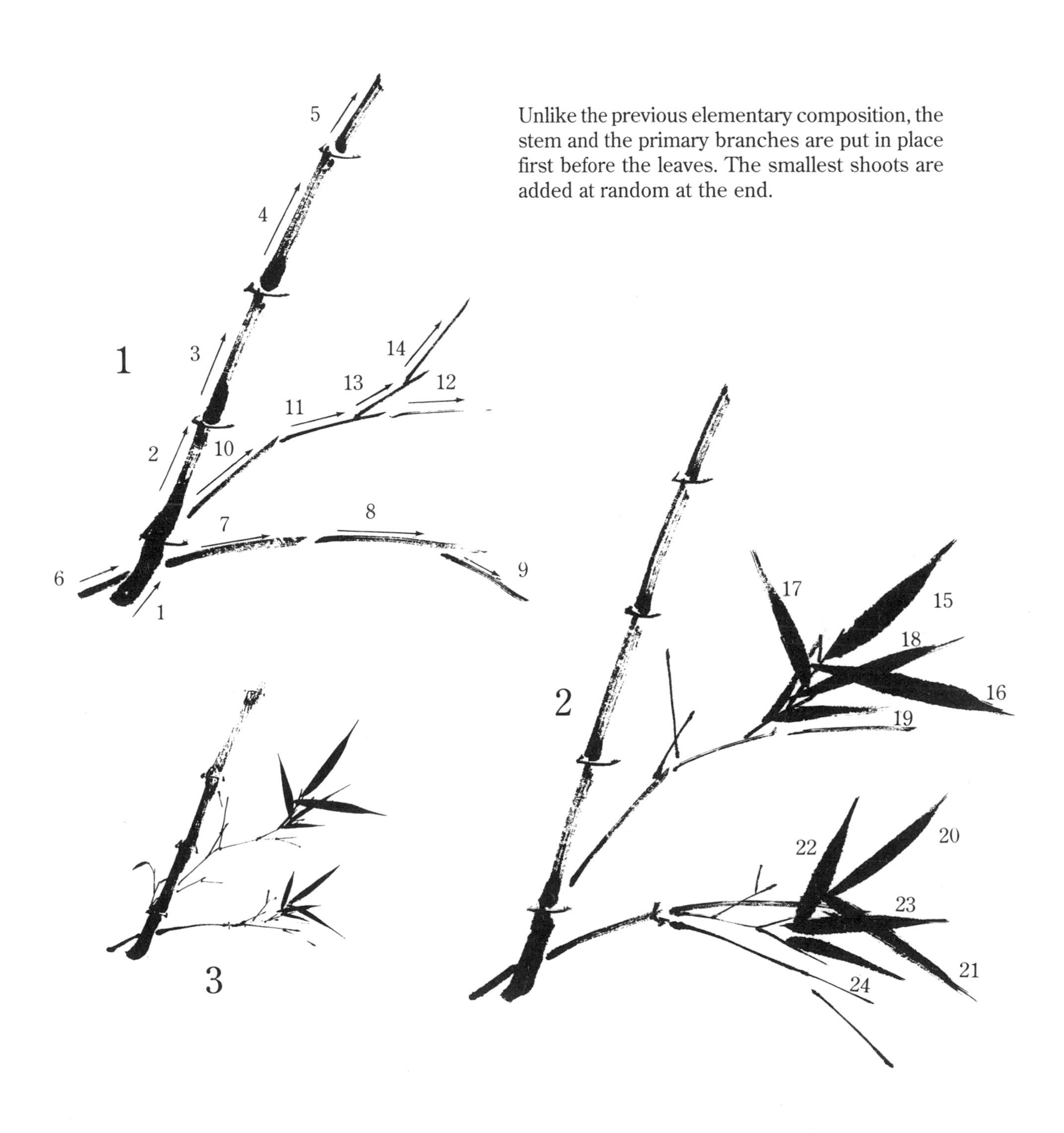

The Drooping Bamboo

The great aesthetic appeal of the bamboo is due in no small measure to the stalwart resilience of its robust stems silhouetted against clusters of lively flapping leaves. These have been likened to the animations of flying birds.

In the renowned *Mustard Seed Garden Manual* (1887–1888), a number of illustrated examples of the bamboo were individually described as: (1) The Swallow's Tail, (2) The Startled Rook, (3) The Wild Goose Alighting and (4) The Swallow in Flight. The four examples given here are copies by the author.

"Therefore, in painting the bamboo, one must have a good idea of the subject in one's chest. With brush in hand, one concentrates on visualizing an image of what one wants to paint. Then swiftly following the idea, one would pursue it with the brush like the hawk swooping down on a bolting rabbit. With a moment's hesitation, it would be lost."***

—From a well-known treatise on the art of painting the bamboo attributed to Wen Tong (1018–1079), reported by his pupil Li Xi Zhai*** as his advice to Su Dong Bo, one of China's greatest writers and poets noted for his bamboo paintings.

* The expression "bamboo in the chest" has become a widely known idiom meaning that one is well-planned for the situation.

** Translation from the original by the author.

*** Part of Li's *Treatise on the Bamboo* is quoted at the opening paragraph in the *Book of the Bamboo* of the *Mustard Seed Garden Manual.*

The Steps in Drawing The Drooping Bamboo Leaves (Types 2 and 3)

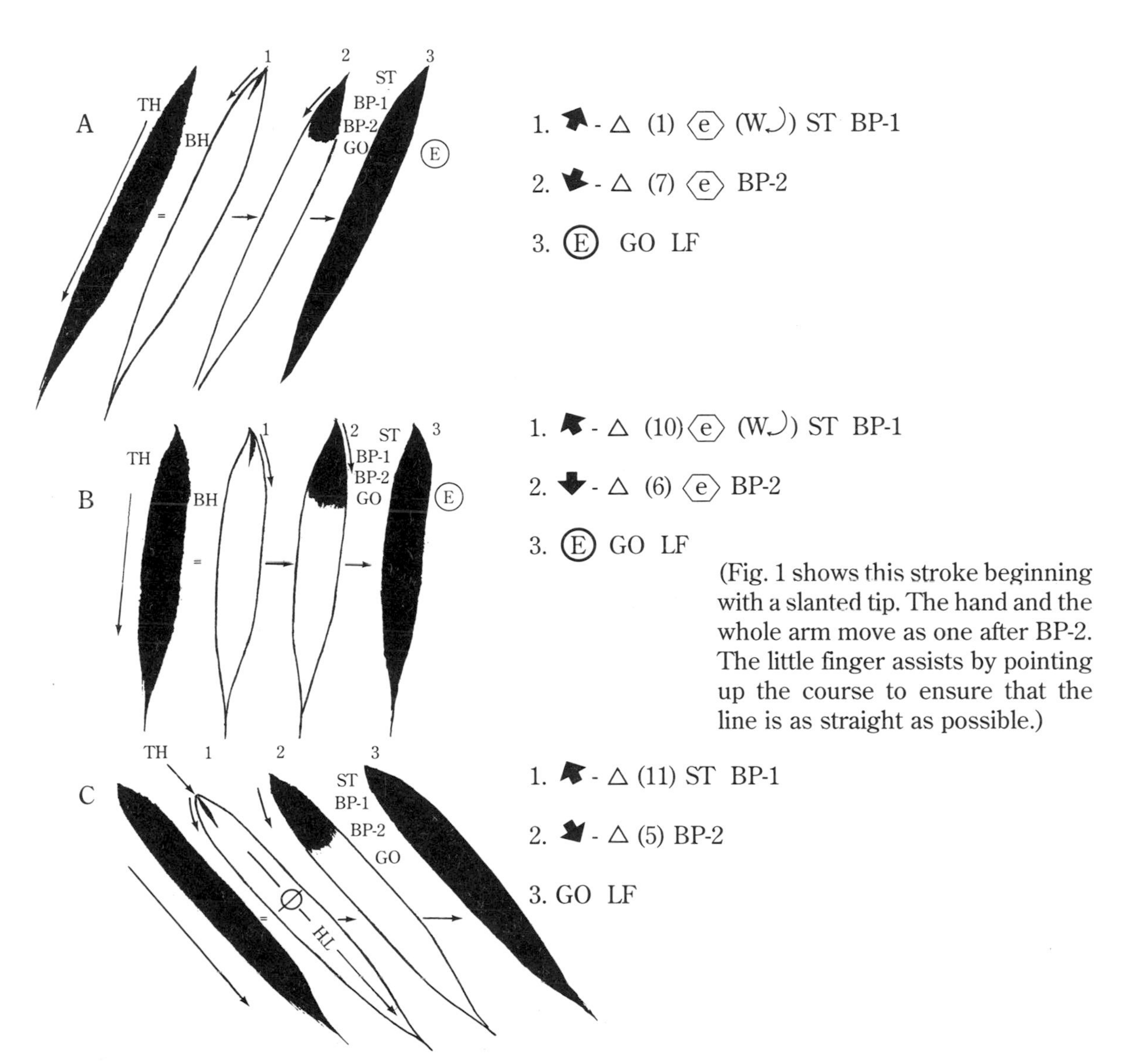

W and Ⓔ are not shown on fig. C3. In this case, the hand folds back at the wrist with the whole arm moving in unison. Where the head is not turned sideways as in figure B, the tip remains in the center of the stroke, similar to the sunshine bamboo leaves.

Anatomy of The Drooping Bamboo Leaf

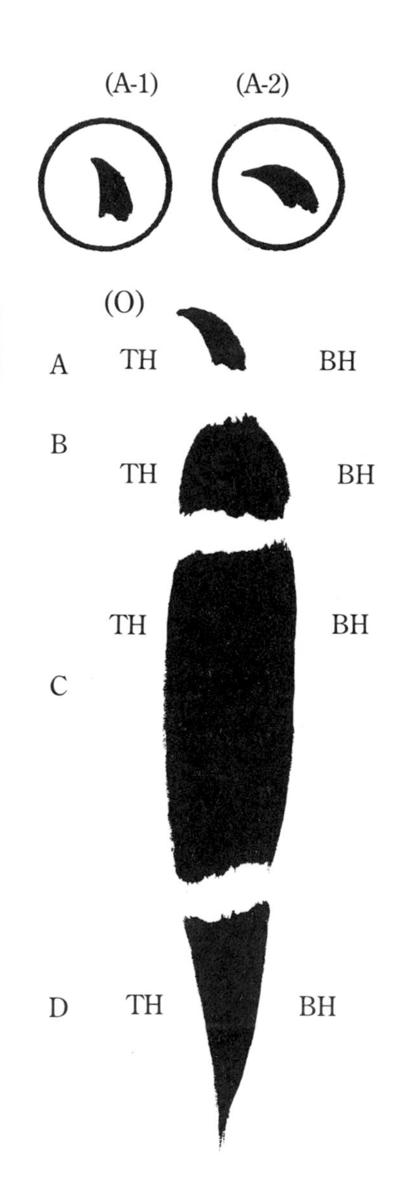

(A-1) and (A-2) are variations of (A).

(O) Tip of the brush is extended to this point before it is set down to begin the downstroke at (A). The hand is tilted upward while the wrist remains in the pivotal position preparatory to making the W↷ turn to start the long journey down from (A).

(A) (10) W↷. Use tip hairs only, no pressure.

(B) Wrist makes W↷ turn and leans on the belly hairs—(BH/ST/BP-1/BP-2). This movement widens the stroke here, as shown. The W↷ turn is aborted on reaching the desired width at the end of (B).

(C) The forearm is activated. Keep the eyes on the line traced by the TH while maintaining a constant pressure on the BH. Do not exert any pressure on the TH which will be trailing somewhat behind the BH. The line on the TH can be regulated by adjusting the pressure sideways on the BH.

(D) Here the elbow takes the weight off the hand as the former begins to raise the brush upward and backward at a deliberate pace. Meanwhile the wrist makes a final W↷ turn accompanied by the gradual elevation of the handle to a more upright position. The TH is shifted back to the center of the line to join up with the BH.

A well-proportioned tail end of the overhanging bamboo leaves is an important feature of painting the bamboo in the "boneless" style. The following are two primary factors essential in the depiction of the pointed tail of the drooping leaves:

1. A momentary pressure is exerted by the wrist on the tip hairs in the form of a determined roll W⤸ while the elbow moves up and away from the table in the split second before the brush clears the painting surface.
2. Natural water tension combines with the resilient nature of the "wolf hairs" to draw the loose strands of the tuft together to form the pointed tip once the pressure is released.

The conclusion drawn from (2) is that the amount of ink loaded on the brush should be closely monitored at all times; overloading would cause the hairs to disperse, while underloading would result in the depletion of water content. Either condition is counter-productive. Finally, a word on the figures A, A-1 and A-2, which involve action by the tip only without moving the wrist from its opening W⤸ position. Where the curvature of the top line is more pronounced, such as in fig. A-2, the operation is made easier by rolling the handle between the thumb and the index finger as shown by figures X and Y.

1. To turn the line to the right, start with the thumb clutching the handle close to the top of the first phalanx (Fig. X).

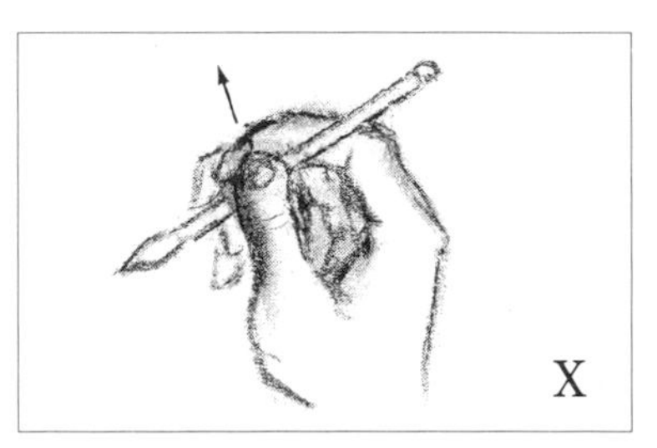

X

2. Push the thumb forward to roll the handle between it and the index finger, which should move back in the opposite direction, followed by the middle and fourth fingers ending in the position shown in Fig. Y.

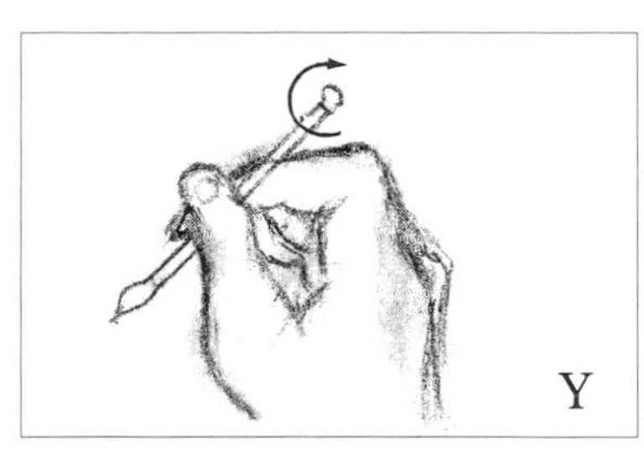

Y

A word of caution: Even though the action described above is only a brief one, the grip of the handle normally carried out by the thumb and the index finger is temporarily released while the "rolling" operation is in progress. It is therefore imperative that the middle and fourth fingers should tighten their hold on the brush until the whole action is completed.

Bamboo Leaves with Deflected Heads and Basic Constituent Cluster Forms

(A) and (B) indicate leaves with deflected heads.
G-1 to G-3 represent common cluster building unit forms.

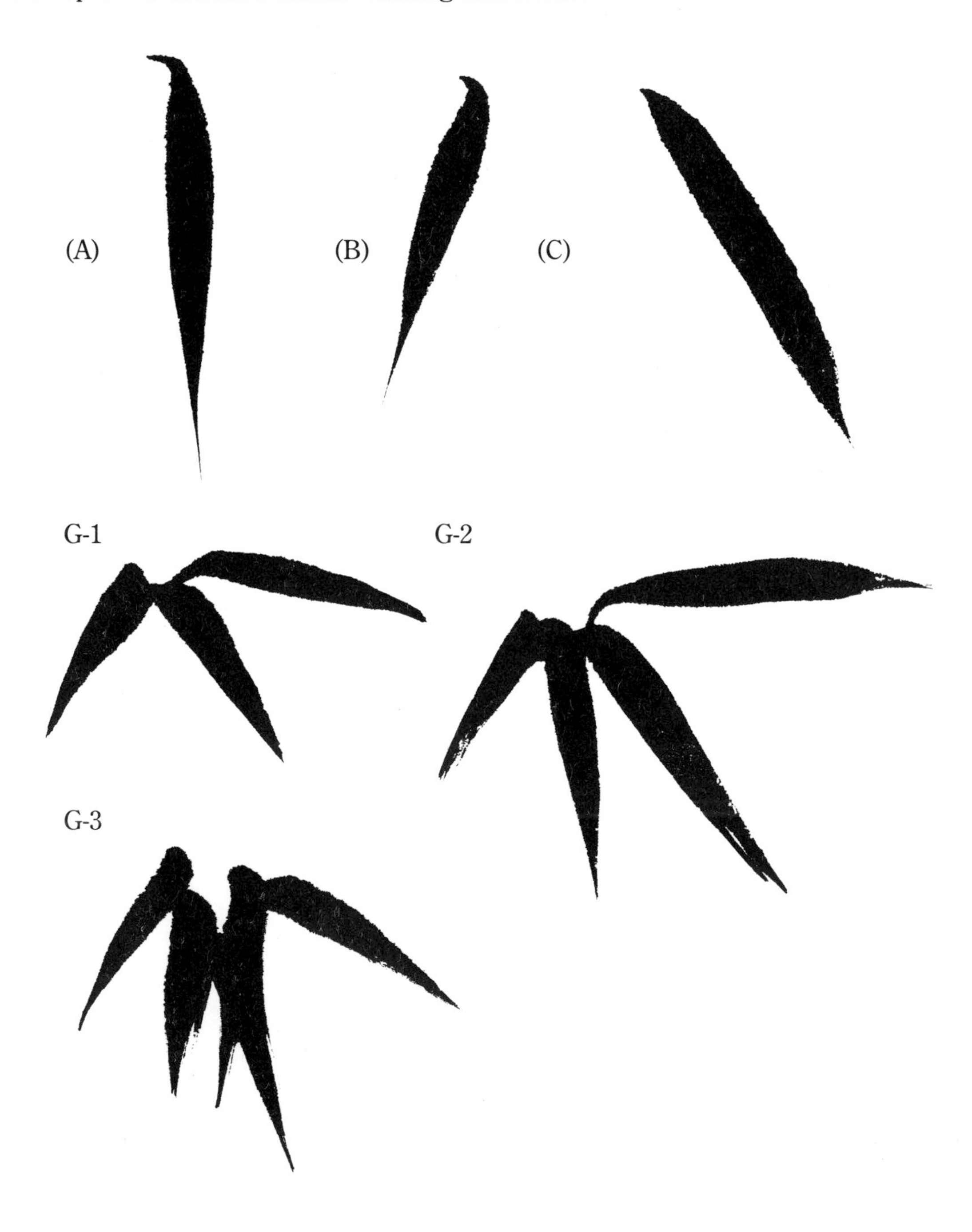

Bamboo Leaves With Deflected Heads And Basic Constituent Cluster Forms

The curved petioles on top of figures A and B on the preceding page represent the part where the leaf joins the twig or branch. When these parts are missing from view, either because they are hidden behind adjacent leaves or because of their great height from the ground, the visible part of the leaf would appear to display a deflected head (see below, examples 1 and 2 in G-1 in addition to leaves 1, 2 and 4 in G-2 as well as leaves 1, 3, 4 and 5 in G-3).

On some of the longer leaves hanging vertically down in the direction of the painter, such as leaf 2 in G-2 and G-3, it may be necessary to move back a few inches from the table to free the forearm from blocking the upsweep of the tip at the final stage where the stroke ends with a sharp point. The problem is most felt when such leaves are positioned near the bottom of the page. The alternative is to turn the body sideways and approach them with the forearm parallel to the bottom line of the paper.

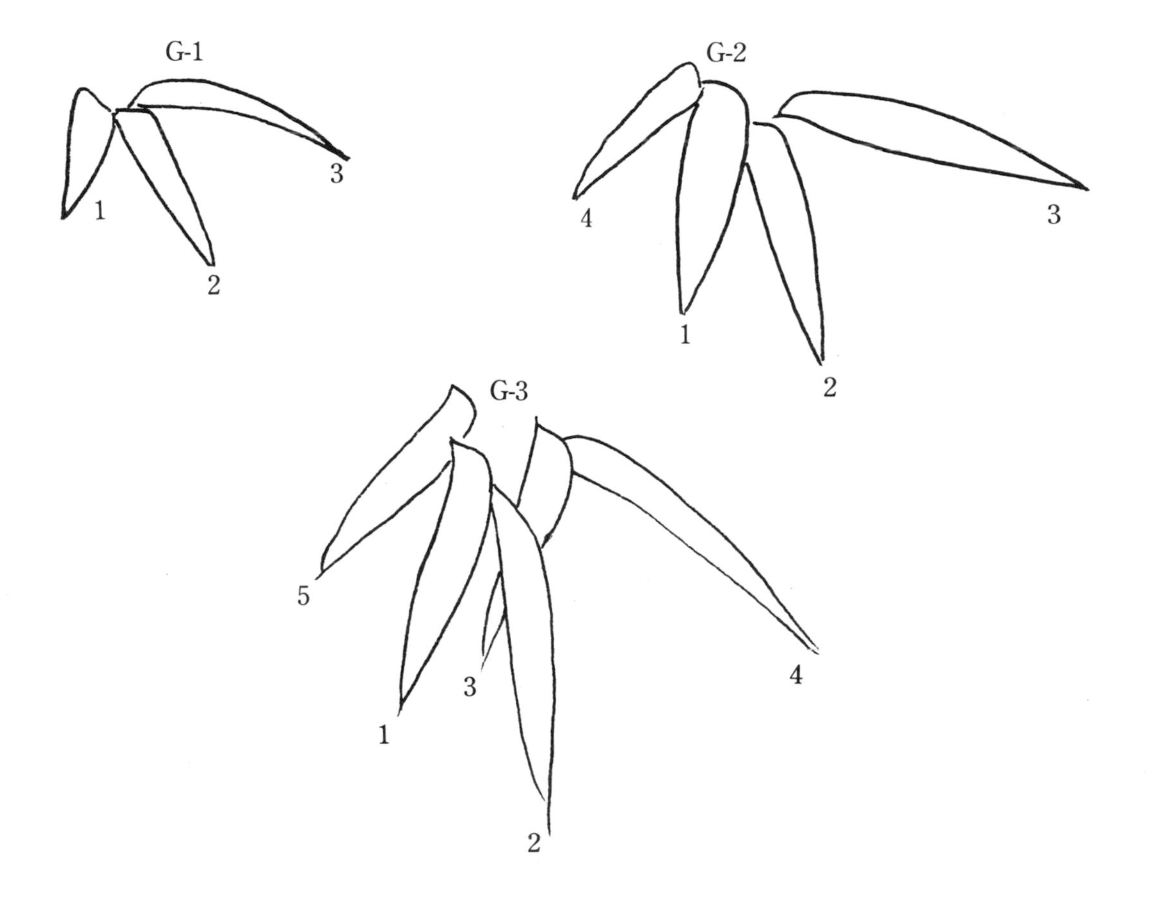

Figures G-1, G-2 and G-3 on the preceding page are outlined copies of the clusters shown in the section "Bamboo Leaves with Deflected Heads and Basic Constituent Cluster Forms." The numbers signify the order in which each leaf is set down as part of a group. Only exception: those marked 3 and 4 in G-2 as well as the leaves indicated by the numbers 3 and 5 in G-3 may be reversed according to individual preference.

As self-contained units, all three examples can appear alone without physical attachment to other clusters. However, they may also be combined with other basic units to form larger conglomerate groups with endless variations in shapes and sizes.

These outlined examples may be used as models to practice the composition of basic group forms by filling in the blanks using only one stroke to paint over each leaf. This, in fact, is one of the standard methods of teaching elementary calligraphy in China. However, do not begin the exercise until you have extra copies made of the original. Once the blanks are filled in, they cannot be used again.

While practicing the unit group forms, you should pay particular attention to the variations in length and direction of each component leaf within the same group. Of course the examples shown in this book are not the only forms used in Chinese paintings. The important thing is to note the deliberately varied treatment of the dimensions of each individual member within a group, which is a classical motif of the art of traditional Chinese painting.

Bamboo with Drooping Leaves (Type 2)

Bamboo with Drooping Leaves (Type 2)

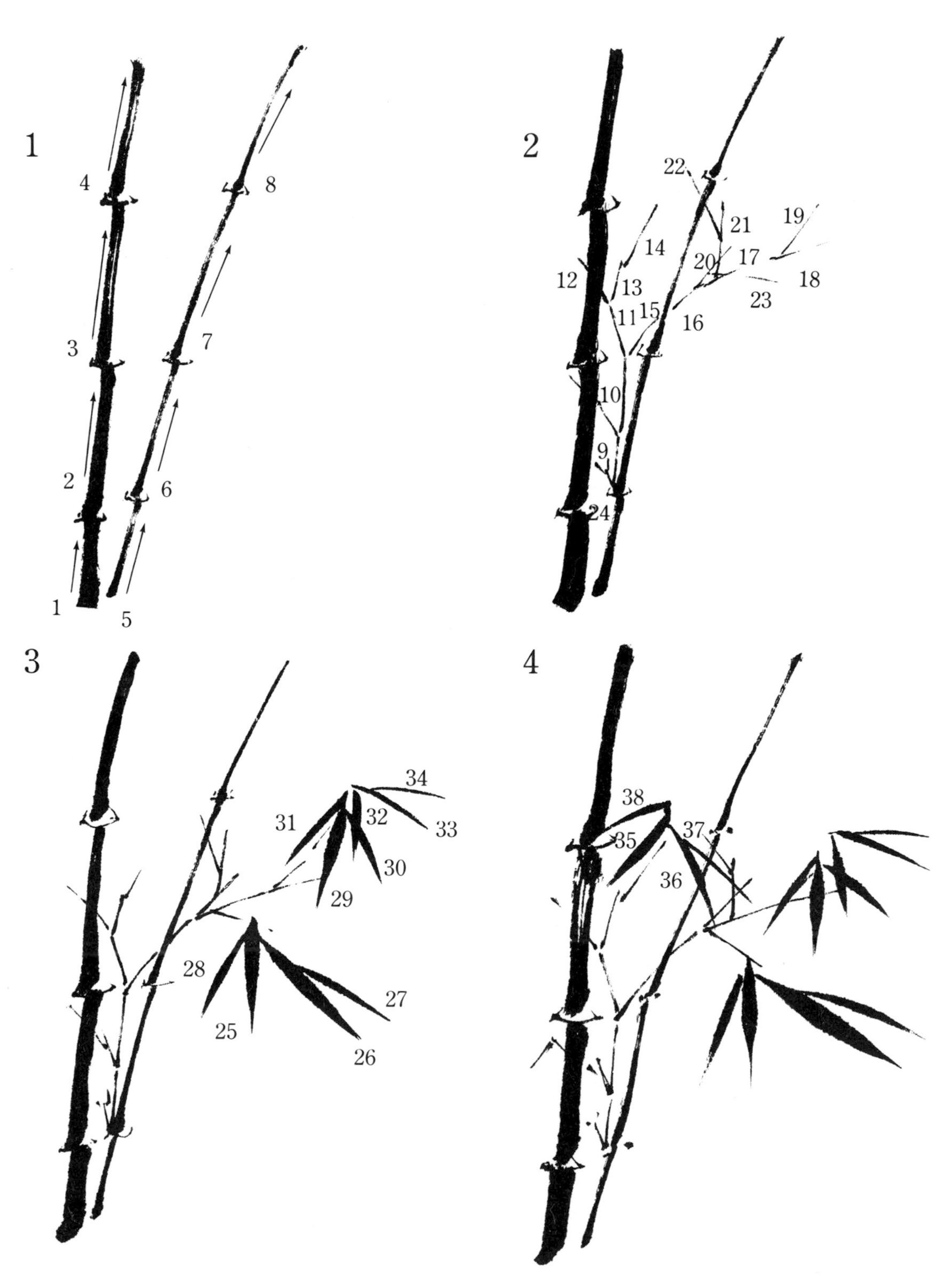

Type two double-loading with the Background-Wash brush

The tuft of the Background-Wash brush is one inch wide, the smallest size available. It is good for painting bamboo stems of about the same width on paper. This kind of brush projects best the well-rounded image of a bamboo through three-dimensional representation. The process is carried out in four simple steps:

1. Completely immerse a clean brush in a very light mixture.
2. Wipe the leading part of the tuft to remove excess ink.
3. To show darker shades on both sides of the stroke, tilt the handle to one side and dip only the corner hairs into dark, undiluted ink. Repeat the same procedure on the other corner (see 1 and 2).
4. Set the brush vertically down on the paper and start painting without hesitation. Be careful not to change the stance or posture of the brush all the way through till the end of the stroke. At the very end, lift the brush straight up to make a clean break off the paper (3). Then start the next section and continue as far as the inkload permits. Do not double-load a second time.

Where two sections meet in linear junction, leave only enough space for the ridge marks to fill in the gaps. On stems up to one inch wide, dip the brush into dark ink mixture well below one-quarter of an inch, measured from the tip of the corner hairs lowered straight into the mixture.

If you follow the above directions, you can look forward to an easy-going time in your very first endeavors to draw an eye-catching bamboo stem in three dimensions.

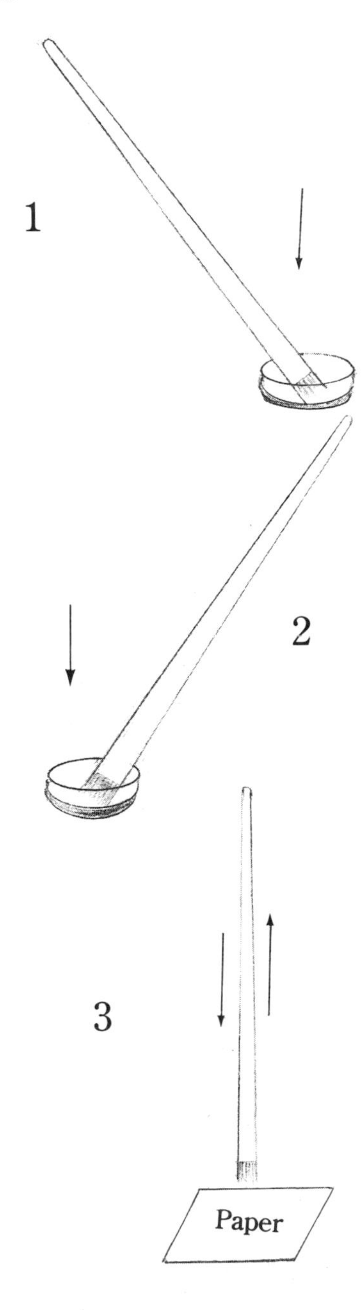

Figures 1 and 2 show how the brush may be loaded twice to produce a two-sided shading effect as shown in "The Drooping Bamboo, Type 3."

The Drooping Bamboo (Type 3)

Details of the Drooping Bamboo (Type 3)

Notable differences between this example and Type 2:

1. The flat Background-Wash brush is used on the stem to produce darker shades on both sides.
2. Lighter ink mixture on two groups of leaves (Figures D and E) provides color tone contrast over the rest of the clusters.

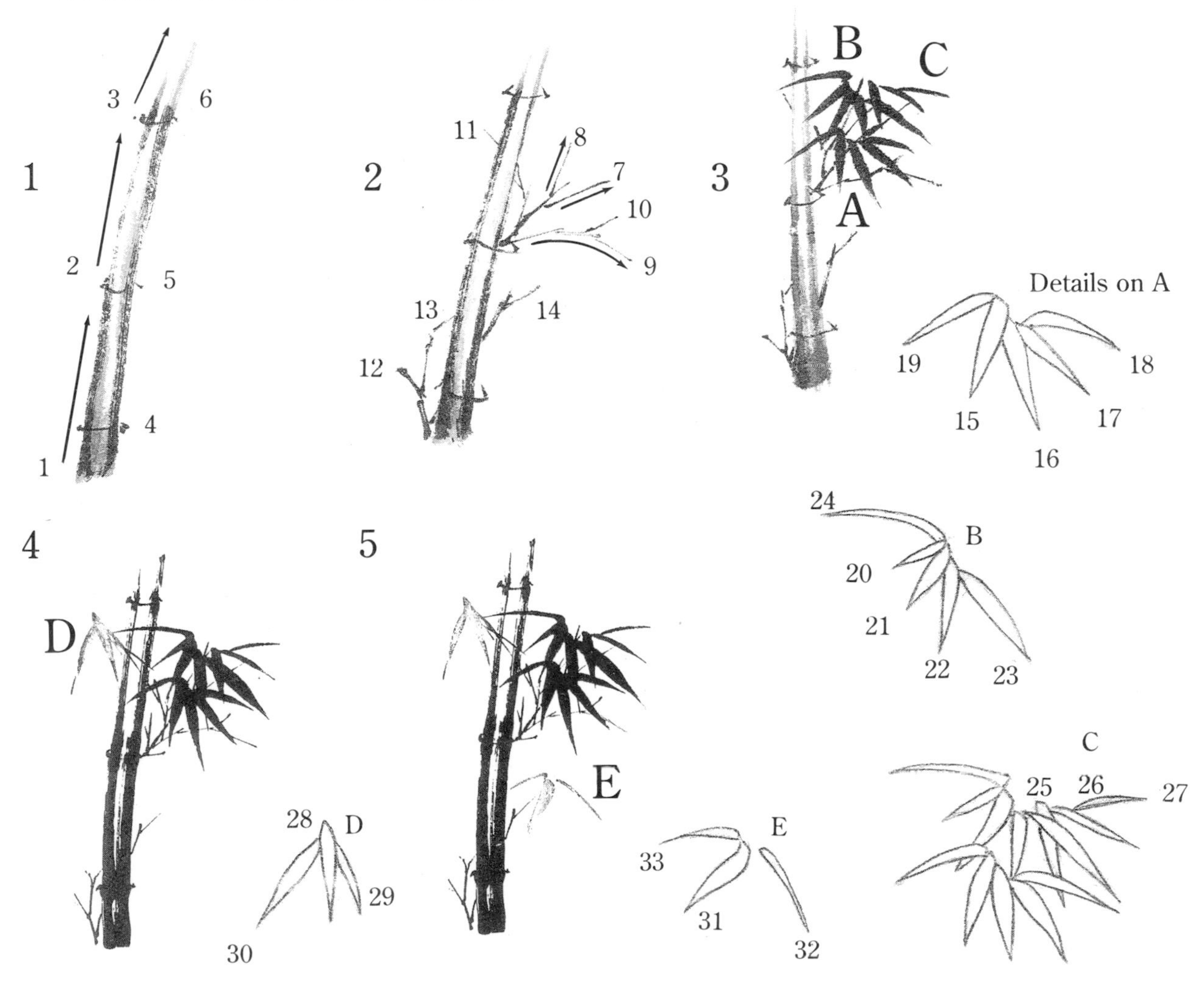

THE PLUM

Many kinds of plum trees of the genus *Prunus Mume* are found in China, some bearing white blossoms and others, green or pink. All of them are noted for their ability to bloom in the middle of winter, alone among all flowering trees. As a popular symbol of long and vigorous life which flourishes even in sub-zero temperature, the plum is painted only in winter dress: never in leaf, because its cycle of growth is programed in such a way that the prime of florescence is already deciduous when the leaves start to show in early spring. Since this usually happens around New Year's time, particularly in the warmer regions in the south of the country, it is also seen as bringing renewed hope to mankind during the festive season, much in the same spirit as expressed in the well-known line, "If Winter comes, can Spring be far behind?"

The globular shape of the plum petals requires an entirely different mode of brushwork from that which is used to draw simple straight lines such as the type prescribed in the previous chapter for the bamboo. In addition, a smoothly co-ordinated wrist action involving even parts of the hand and the arm is indispensable in the treatment of the classical motif of interweaving branches in traditional Chinese paintings of the plum tree.

Unlike the bamboo stems, the trunks and branches of the plum are not straight, except for the young shoots. Five graded shades of ink tones (A to E on the following page) are used for different parts of the plant: A and B at the diluted end of the chromatic scale are indicated for the trunk and the petals, while E, the darkest shade, is for the shoots, moss dots, calyxes and stamens. That leaves C and D for the majority of branches in the middle spectra. The upright hold is generally applied when drawing the branches, with the tip of the brush kept largely in the center of the stroke. (See examples A and C for faint trace of hair line down the center.)

The plum tree is noted for its rugged trunks and the frequent crossing of its branches. Three common types of bifurcation are given overleaf: (Y), which is shaped like the letter "y;" (X), which is plainly identifiable with the letter "x;" and finally (G), which is described as the "girl" type of crossing because of its resemblance to the "girl" symbol in an ancient script arranged in the form of a female with crossed legs*. The "girl" character shown here is based on the style of the archaic Li-Shu script prevalent during the Han dynasty (206 B.C.–A.D. 219). The difference between X and G lies in the fact that the two arms of the latter move along increasingly divergent directions. The gap between strokes 3 and 4 is a space left open to be filled in later with plum blossoms.

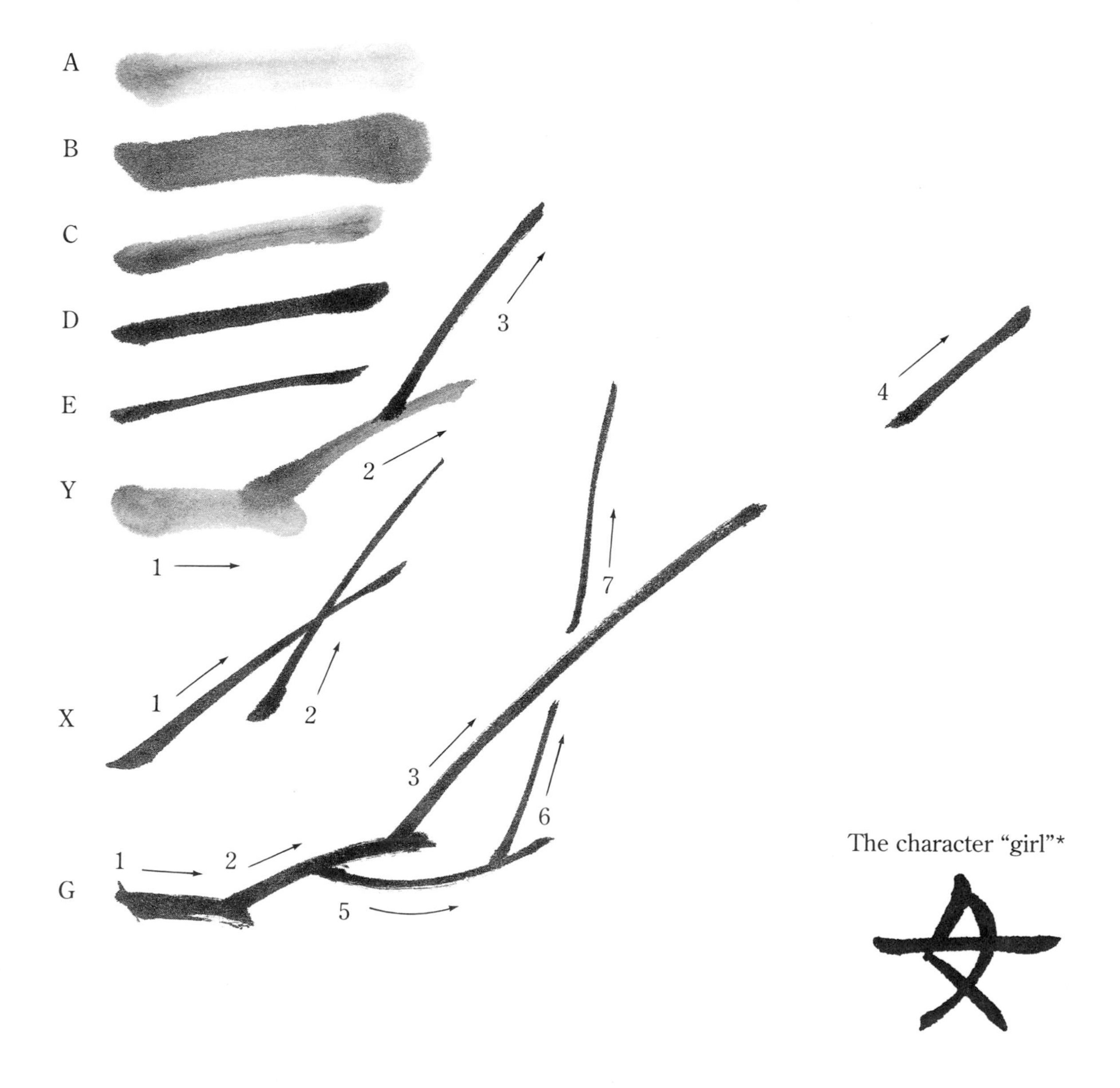

The character "girl"*

* Reference to the "girl" element as an important technique in the art of painting the plum can be found in many past treatises on the subject, including the celebrated *Mustard Seed Garden Manual.*

Common Plum Branch Crossing Types

Plum Branchings Displaying X, Y and G Formations

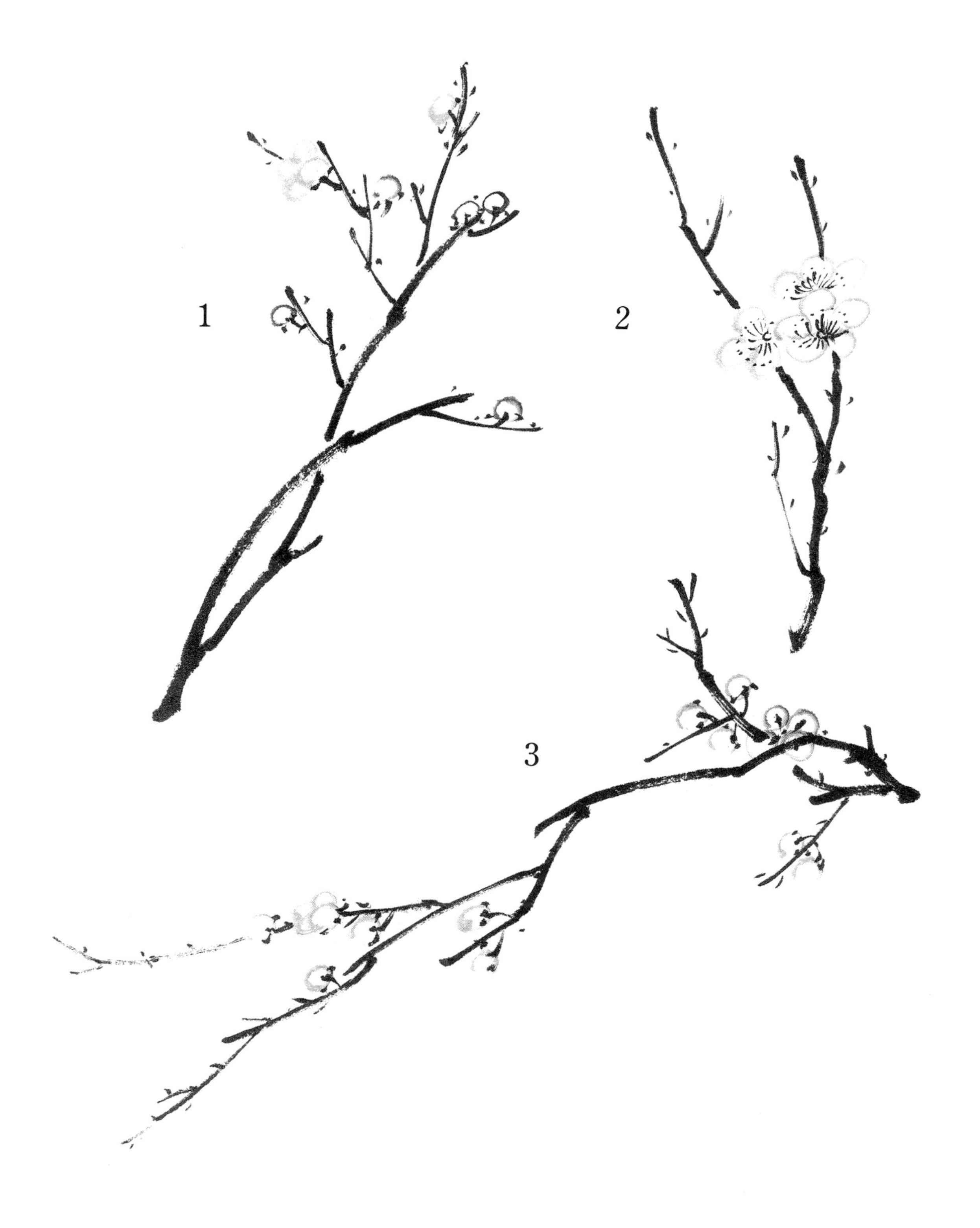

Plum Blossoms

The development of branching ramifications of the plum tree shown in the preceding page is detailed in the following graphic representations:

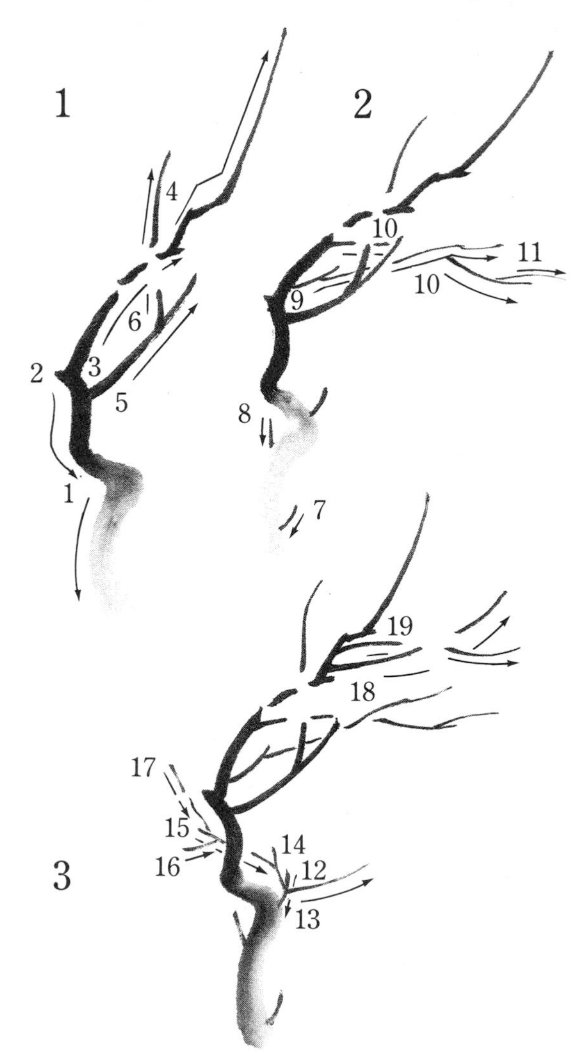

1	P ◣ - ◁ (11) W◡ Φ (dilute mixture)
2	Same as above
3	P ◤ - ◁ (9) ◟W Φ (darker mixture)
4 – 6	Same as above with modifications
7 – 8	See 1 and 2. Use darker ink on both strokes and graft to lower part of trunk before the ink there is completely dry.
9 – 11	Similar to strokes 4 to 6.
12	Same as 7.
13	Similar to 5.
14	Downstroke toward 5 o'clock.
15	Downstroke toward 4 o'clock.
16	Upstroke to the right.
17	Downstroke similar to 8.
18	Similar to 13.
19	Similar to 10.

In traditional paintings of the plum, branches (except for the terminal shoots) are not straight but curved. As a rule, the upstroke is used in painting branches or trunks moving toward 12 to 2 o'clock. On downward or leftward strokes, the downstroke is the norm. In the areas marked by arrows 1 and 2 in (1), portions of the trunk move to the left at the very outset. Hence the downstroke before reaching 3. Note that gaps occur where two or more branches criss-cross so that blossoms bunched together may be displayed with lively variegated postures.

花王圖

菊残猶有傲霜枝
壬子冬日 宗海

The Allure of Plum Blossoms in Simple Settings

Generations ago, the precursors of the art of Chinese brushwork perfected a unique style of reflecting the quintessence of the simple beauty of the plum blossoms using only a minimum of brushwork. This has never since been surpassed. A nascent bud is deftly represented by a semi-circle in one continuous brushstroke. To paint a slightly more mature bud, only a small loop needs to be added alongside the former to complete the transformation from one phase of growth to another. The same basic treatment is applied even to full-blown blossoms consisting of four or five petals set around the heart of the flower. In such cases, each petal in a cyclic arrangement naturally assumes a specific posture different from that of the rest of the ensemble.

In the examples given later, you will find a variety of mature blossoms placed in different postures. In most situations, the group consists of two or three separate modes based upon their respective linear depth measurement from the point of view of the spectator looking from the outside—such as whether a particular petal (or petals) is located in the background (BG in the examples), the middle ground (MG) or foreground (FG). The exception is on flowers set in the upright position in full view of the observer; all four or five petals would be of approximately the same size and dimension then. In a setup where a blossom is set in the supine mode leaning away from the foreground, the front petal would appear comparatively larger than those at the back, while the ones behind would have their surface areas reduced in size. To emphasize the need for positioning different layers of petals in their proper perspective, graded percentages of surface areas of each petal in a group are given alongside some of the examples of mature blossoms as convenient visual guides.

Where a number of mature blossoms burgeon in close proximity, it is more aesthetic to alter the relative arrangements of the petals so that each flower would appear to be turned in a different direction from that of its immediate neighbors. Thus, some petals in the illustrations have been classified as having a "dominant" status when they are placed in the more prominent positions over and above the "sub-dominant" ones. Either a single petal or as many as three may belong to the dominant mode; but it does not necessarily mean that it should consist of a larger surface exposure area. The significance of assigning dominant status to petals in certain positions will be apparent when these are graphically shaded to set them off against the remainder of their group, as shown in the next section.

When is a Circle not a Circle?

The monk Ren Ji of the Yuan dynasty (1279–1368) once said that it took him 40 years of arduous practice to achieve a perfect roundness in his plum petals. Yet the *Mustard Seed Garden Manual* states that plum blossoms should not be drawn in the form of precise circles, one of the 36 "errors" in plum painting. So the student may be justified to ask, "When is a circle not a circle?"

While the outlines on the petals should be smooth and rounded, particularly at the turns, neither the petals nor the complete flower are to be depicted as perfect circles. Given the great variety of postures of the flowers in paintings of the plum, the individual shapes of the petals are as varied as the stances of the flowers in full bloom. The best way to study the plum petals is to start with the simple form of a single petal—not that of a nascent bud, which is basically a modified circlet, but a typical mature petal such as the magnified specimen shown here, divided into five technical areas marked 1 to 5*. There is a zero at the center

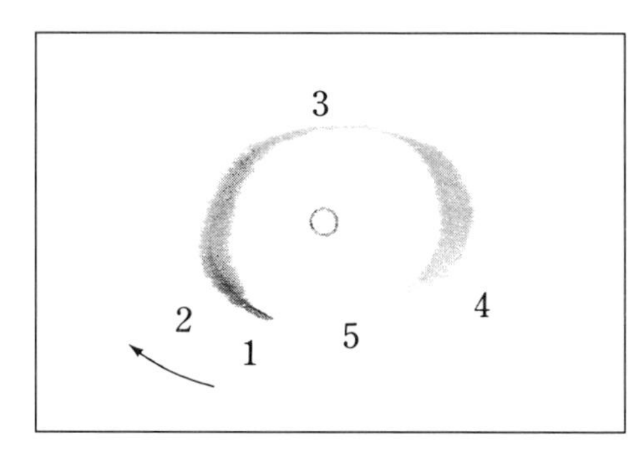

of the figure: this is where the brush is to be pointed vertically in order to secure a point of reference before it is set down to begin painting. From that position, the top of the handle is slanted forward and the tip is shifted backward in the opposite direction so that, as the brush is lowered onto the paper at 1, the tip is correctly postured to begin the stroke with a sharp point. As the brush moves up the left side of the petal, from 1 to 2, the handle is straightened to the vertical position and held there all the way through 4. The ascent from 1 to 2 and beyond is regulated by the middle and fourth fingers working in close co-ordination with the wrist, the latter turning in a clockwise direction (W⤸).

Approaching the summit at 3, the thumb joins the other two fingers to hold firmly onto the brush as the tip hairs change direction, moving toward the other half of the incomplete ellipse. From 4 onward, the stroke enters its most crucial sector; the brush has to be pulled back at an awkward angle, with the handle slanted down again in order to point the tip forward in the direction of 5 before lift-off at the close of the action.

* Note the highlighting effect near the top where the line becomes thinner as the tip is pointed upward and away from the starting point. The heavier lines on the side heighten the illusion that the surface of the petals is not even or flat. It also has the effect of making the subject appear closer to an ellipse than a circle.

To display the flowers in all sorts of interesting postures, they may be set down at selected, strategic positions even before the branches are brought in to give support. Consequently, there are no prescribed orders as to how and when the blossoms should be taken care of, once the trunk and a few primary branches are in place. Many of the smaller branches or twigs are added at random as the need arises.

Below is an example of bringing a branch to a blossom drawn in advance.

Before After

Plum Blossoms in Various Sizes and Postures

Strokes on the filaments under (a) move downward or upward to the right. Strokes under (b) move downward between 7 and 3 o'clock. Strokes under (c) move upward to the right. In the third column, numbers 1 to 5 indicate the sequences of painting*. For right-handed persons the natural tendency is to move from left to right as indicated by the arrows. However, both the directions and the numbers may occasionally be modified if the postures of the blossoms are tilted heavily into other modes not shown here. The filaments together with the anthers are referred to collectively as stamens.

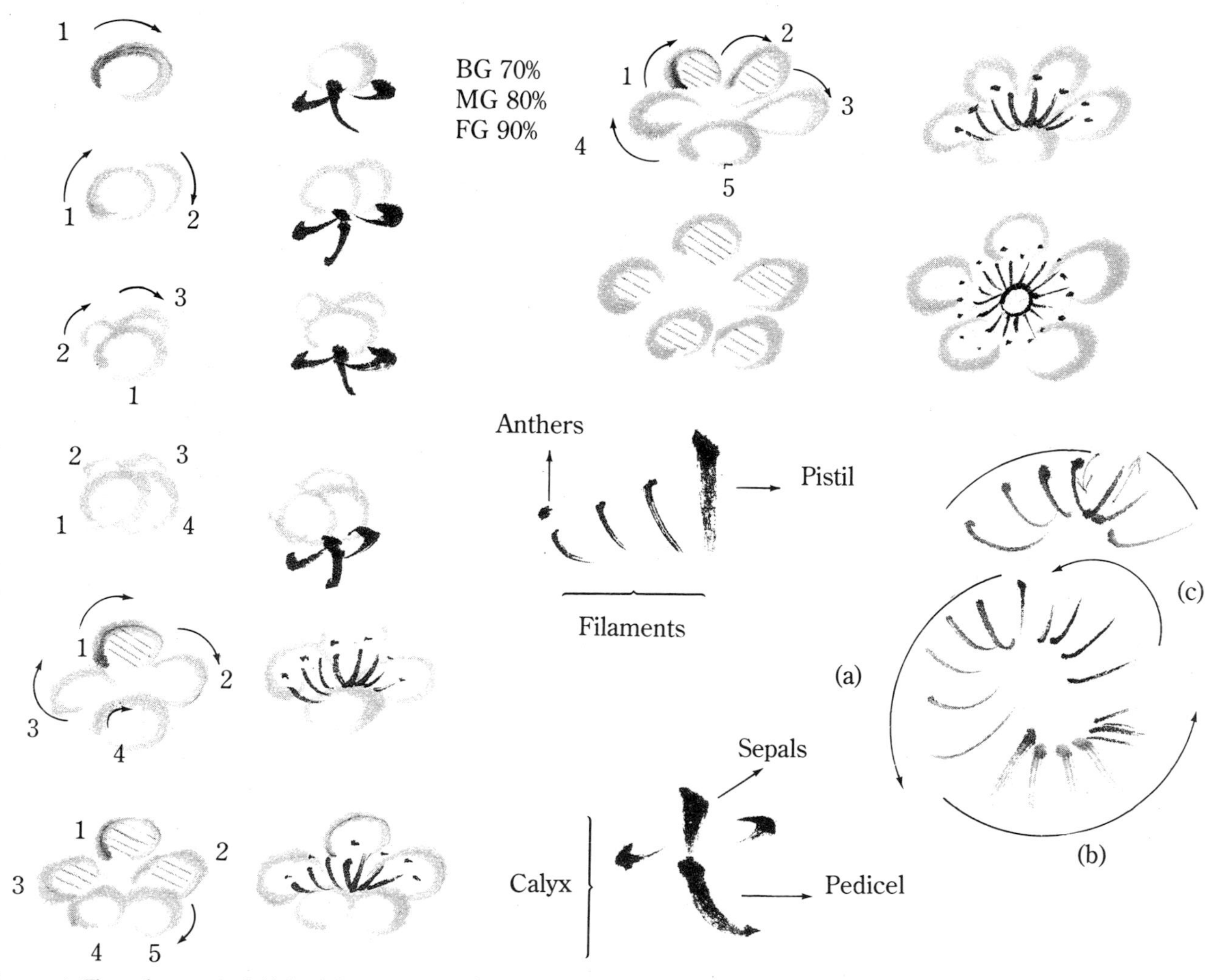

* The orders are for initial training purposes only. By following them, it is possible to ensure that the ensuing number partly overlaps the previous one around the intersecting areas so as to leave no doubt about their relative position in the scheme of things. Once adept in the proper placement of the petals, the orders can be reversed by drawing the anterior ones first.

Examples of Petals Set in the Foreground, Middle Ground and Background

A

C

E

B

D

F

Plum Blossoms in Mo-ku ("Boneless") Painting

Plum blossoms in Mo-ku painting
Example 2 shows a blossom set down without any apparent physical support according to the practice of prior emplacement of projected blossoms. In example 3, the missing support is provided by the meandering limb extending from one of the primary boughs seen in 1. Finally, the buds, anthers, sprigs, moss dots and so on are brought in in example 4.

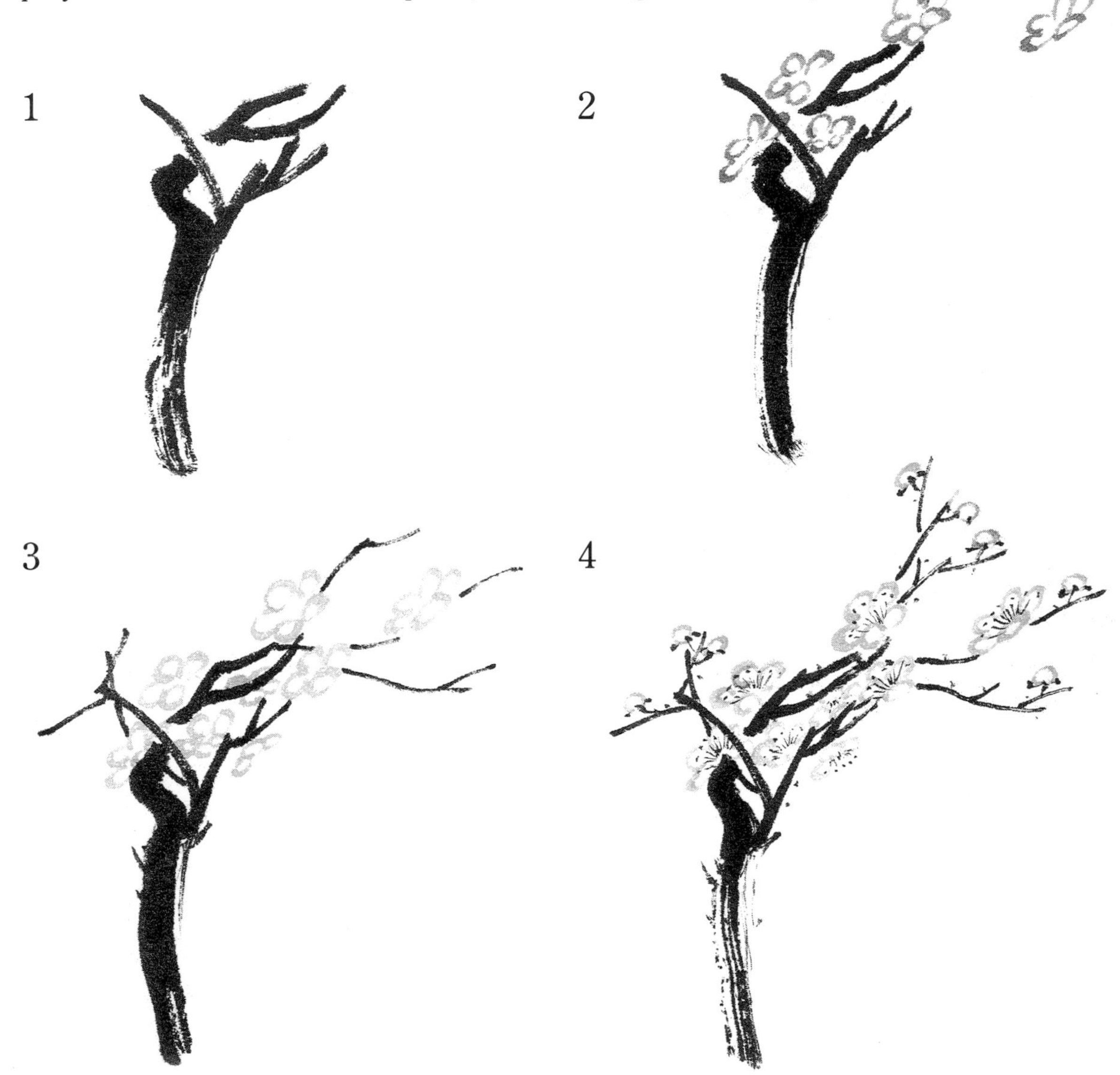

Note: Because of the reduced dimension of the examples, the outlined mode of painting the petals in lieu of the Mo-ku style is applied on the flowers only.

Loading the brush for Mo-ku petals

1 Rinse the brush in clear water before each loading.
2 Wipe it over a piece of paper towel to remove excess moisture up to about half the length of the tuft measured from the tip.
3 Dip it in a very dilute mixture to half the depth.
4 Clear the tip of the dilute mixture to make room for the double-loading of a dark, but not dry, ink mixture such as ready-made ink from the bottle. For better control on this second loading, the tip is lowered vertically and immersed to less than one-eighth of an inch.

After the final loading, the brush is charged with three distinct color zones: clear liquid at the base, dilute mixture in the middle, and dark, concentrated ink at the lowest point of the tip. To prevent the black tint from spreading into the area around the heart of the blossom where the stamens are located, the tip is first set down on the upper left side of the petal (position

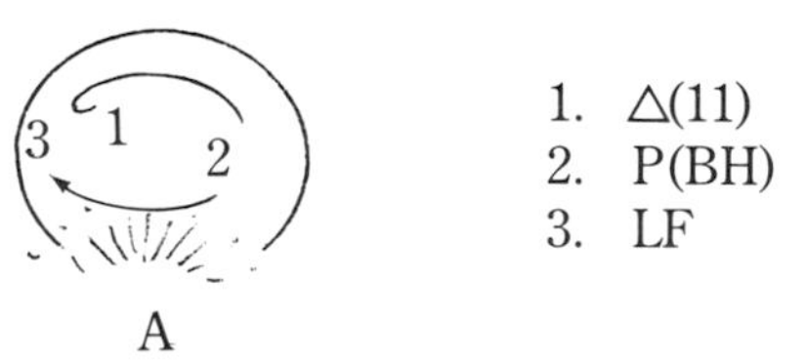

1). The tip is initially pointed at 11 o'clock with the handle held at about 45°. From there the tip makes a brief U-turn to skirt along the perimeter over the top of the petal in a circular movement ending at point 3, shortly before terminating at 1. Throughout this maneuver, the tip remains pointed to the left while a slight pressure on the belly hairs from position 2 onward forces the clear water from the higher level to diffuse over the lower region, delineating a clear, colorless area close to the heart of the complete blossom.

On petals in other postures, the following manipulative modifications are indicated.

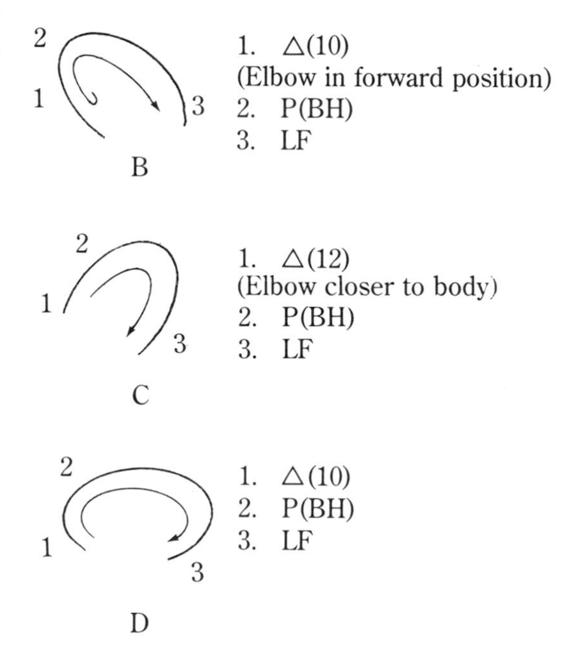

In all four examples, manipulative actions are primarily executed by the fingers with the hand and wrist providing supplementary support where necessary. In general, the handle is held at a more erect angle at the point of impact and slanted from position 2 where pressure (P) is indicated until shortly before position 3.

THE ORCHID

The orchid is the first of the Four Paragons examined in Part II of the *Mustard Seed Garden Manual* in the volume dealing with the four popular plants. The orchid heads the list because it is the first to bloom in early spring. It symbolizes the premier *Qi* (life-breath) of the four seasons—followed by Bamboo (summer), Chrysanthemum (autumn) and Plum (winter). The same arrangement is not followed in this book because, in terms of intricacy of brushwork control, the orchid is technically more complex than the two plants studied in the previous chapters.

The orchids featured in traditional Chinese painting—*Cymbidium Virescens*—do not look quite the same as those commonly found in the West. According to the *Manual*, two generic types are represented in Chinese brushwork: *Lan* and *Hui*. They are also known as grass and marsh orchid. The principal difference between the *Lan* and the *Hui* lies in the fact that the former bears only a single flower per stem, while in the case of the *Hui*, several flowers can grow from the same stalk.

Among the flowering plants most admired in the Orient, the orchid is noted not only for its elegant beauty, but also for the centuries-old belief that its ambrosial fragrance possesses therapeutic values capable of warding off diseases.

Twenty centuries ago, orchids were used to freshen bath water or were worn for sanitation purposes. These observations were recorded in one of the nine elegies entitled *Li Sao,* attributed to the virtuous Minister of the State of Chu, Chu Yuan (4th century B.C.), who committed suicide by drowning. The event is commemorated all over China on the fifth day of the fifth month of the lunar year with the annual staging of the popular Dragon Boat Race.

Found in the wild or in marshes, the orchid is emblematic of pristine nature in its purest form. To intellectual artists who are devoted nature lovers, the orchid is thus the favorite candidate to top the list of the Four Paragons.

Leaves

In any course on orchid painting, the leaves are usually studied first. Of the four examples shown here, begin with the shortest one at the top (A) and move on to (B) and (C) etc., in that order.

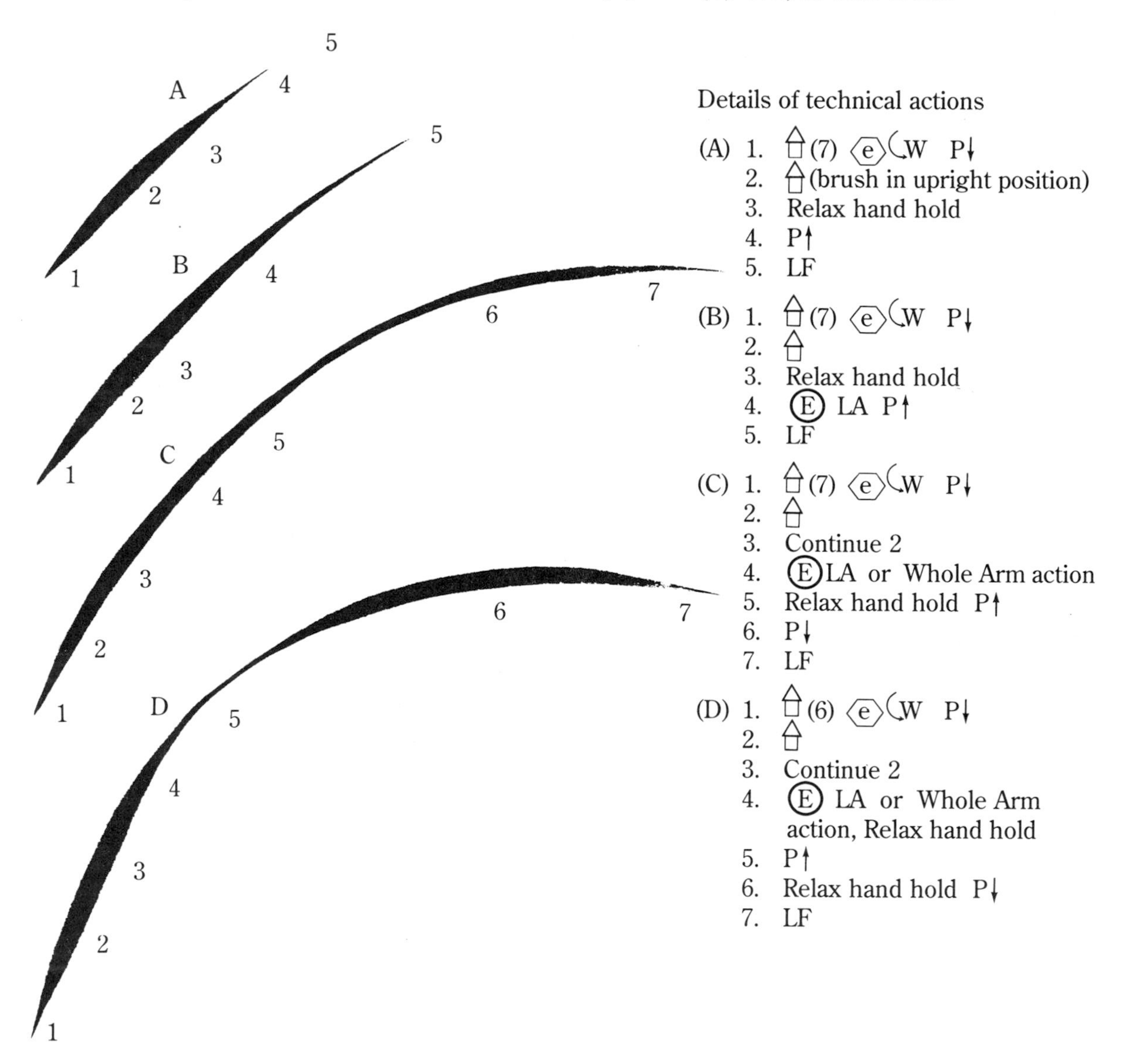

Note: The tip should always remain at the center of the line. Where it widens, the handle should be held firmly. Relax the hand before raising the brush with the arm at P↑. Complete all strokes with a continuous motion. It is easier to paint orchids with very long leaves while standing up. Hold the brush firmly with the thumb and index finger and adjust the height of your grip so that the lower arm is kept horizontal. This helps to keep the brush in the vertical position.

Flowers and buds

Except for their firmer and more delicate texture, the petals of the orchid flowers look very much like a miniaturized version of leaf example (A) given previously. Where several flowers sprout from the same stalk, like in the marsh orchid, the buds, if shown, are positioned at the top of the stems.

At A-1, all four fingers are extended to adjust to the low slanted mode of the tip at point of impact (⌂/12 Φ).

At B-1, the normal grip is used except that here, the palm is turned to the left toward 10 o'clock. The direction of the tip at impact is (⌂/10 Φ).

The Hui

Graded Diagrams of a Hui Orchid

Leaves 6 and 7 are added after the five mature flowers in (2) are painted in between primary leaves 1, 2 and 3 which set the motif of the complete picture. The short leaf no. 8 near the ground is drawn with the downstroke. At the bottom of the plant is a bunch of exposed roots, an optional feature executed with short, meandering strokes using a semi-dry brush charged with light ink mixture.

The Lan (1)

The Lan

Of the two types of orchids, the *Lan* is better known to the general public. The fewer number of flowers recalls the pristine, rarefied environment in which the plant is thought to thrive in remote, secluded areas.

It is not unusual then for a tableau to feature only the barest number of flowers, such as the example on the preceding page (which is the author's copy of an illustration in the *Mustard Seed Garden Manual*). The stroking details are shown below.

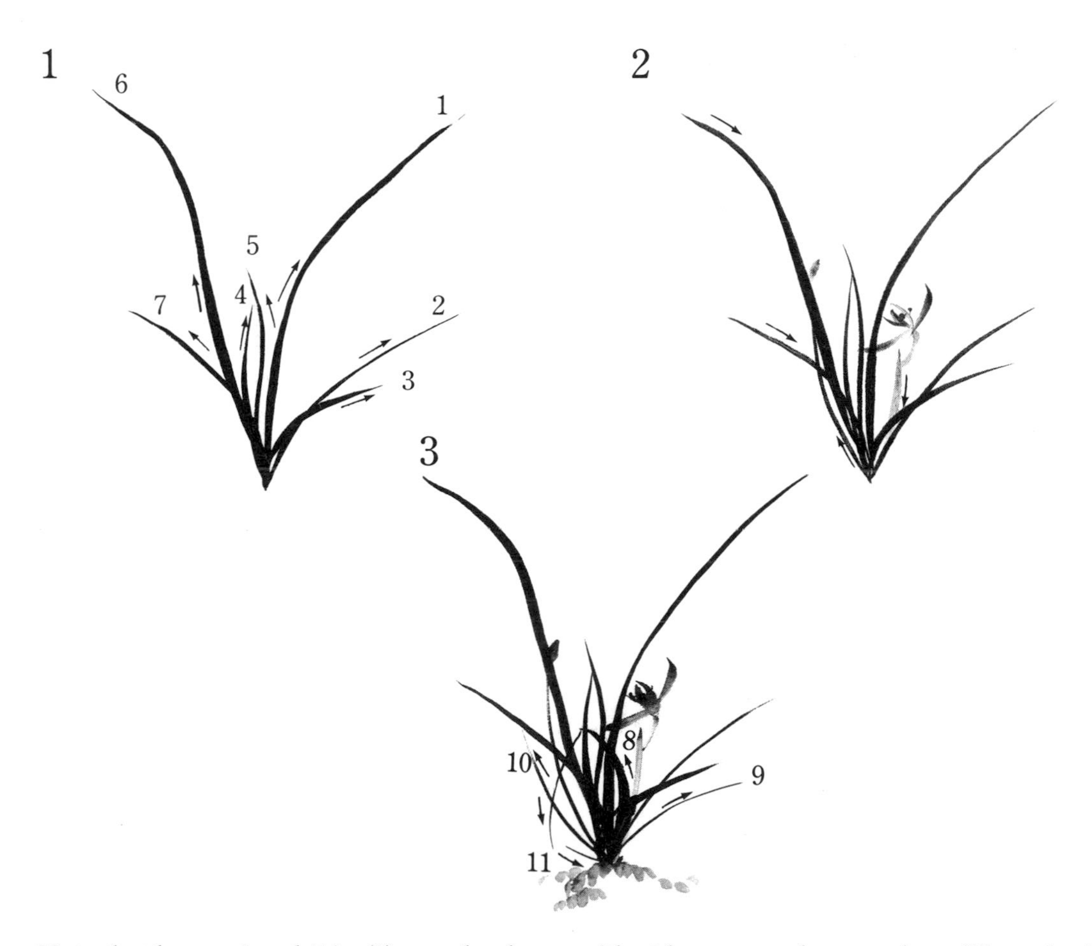

Note that leaves 6 and 7 in (1) may be drawn with either up- or downstrokes. (Upstroke in 1 and downstroke in 2.) Although leaf no. 5 resembles the stem supporting the mature flower in (2), the latter is brought in only after the flower is painted. The stem is done with a downstroke in order to ensure correct alignment between the flower and its root in the ground. On the other hand, the stem for the half-hidden bud is executed with the upstroke since the connection is intersected by an interposing long blade. On (3), the disjointed leaf no. 8 is completed in two separate strokes: the first half with the upstroke and the reverse for the second half. The ground cover can be done according to individual preference.

The Lan (2)

The Steps in Setting Up A Cluster of Twelve Lan Orchid Leaves

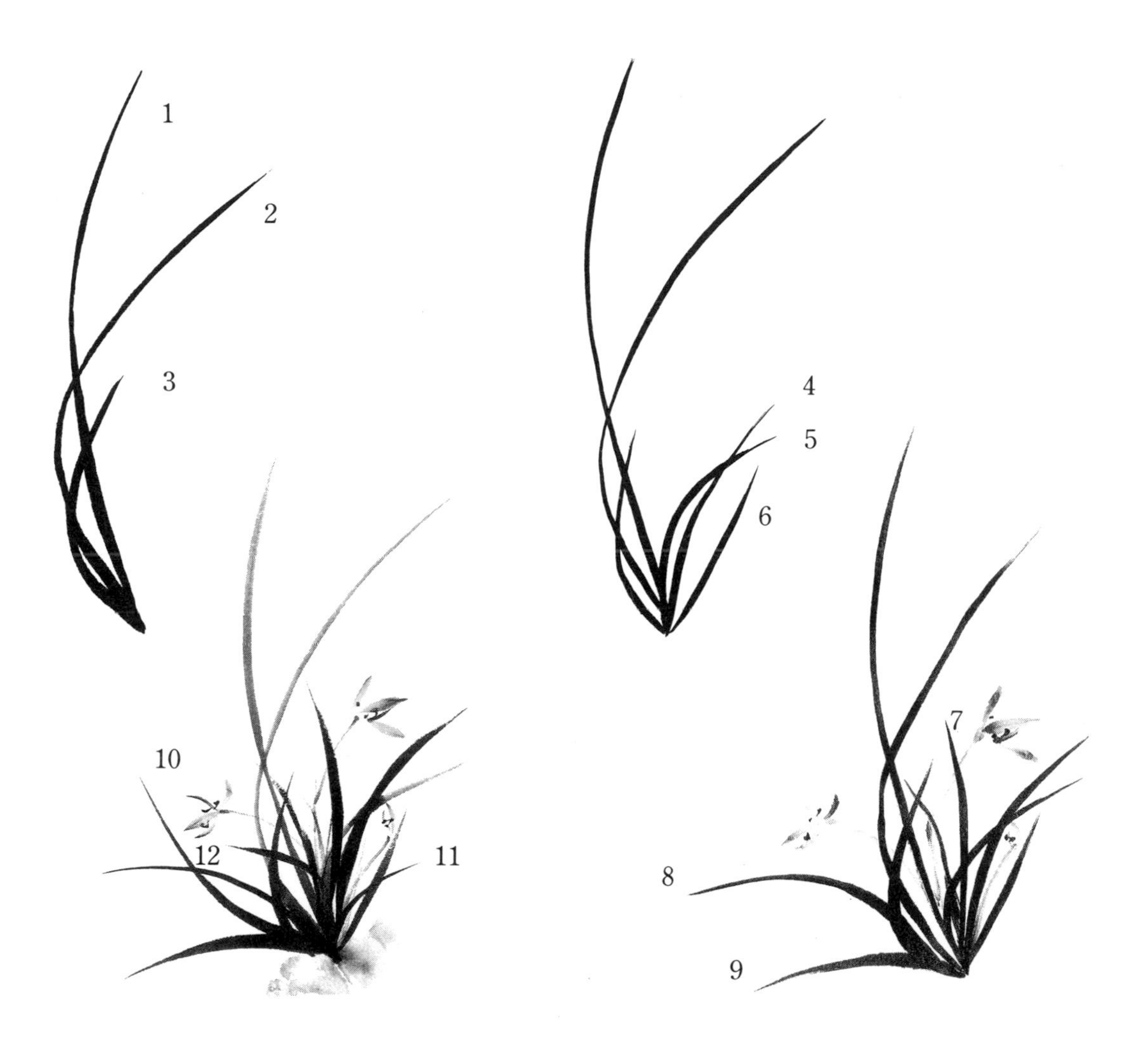

Leaves 10, 11 and 12 may be drawn after the flowers are put in place. The flower at the top is painted first, followed by the one on the left and the half-hidden bud on the right. The stems and a few shorter blades are finally added at random. The petals are drawn with the vertical brush with the tip steadfastly held to the center of the stroke. Once again, the ground cover is optional and done with light, medium mixture and a not overly dry brush. For the petals, all strokes move inward, from the extremities toward the center of the flower.

THE CHRYSANTHEMUM

The chrysanthemum is the last of the Four Paragons to be dealt with in this book. Many varieties of chrysanthemums, with a wide range of shapes and colors are found in traditional Chinese paintings. As the number of cultivated varieties continues to expand, it has become one of the most popular subjects of modern day artists.

The chrysanthemum is indigenous to most of China where it grew as far back as 2500 years ago. The very large genus of annuals and perennials becomes inflorescent in the fall; in the old days, the ninth month of the lunar calender was also known as the "The Month of the Chrysanthemum."

Although more than one hundred and sixty varieties of this plant exist in China alone, Liu Meng of the Song dynasty was able to classify only forty-one types of *mums* in the earliest taxonomic record of its kind. It was during the Song dynasty that poets and artists, inspired by their great beauty, expounded the various styles of painting the giant flowers in pastels of ink and assorted colors.

In recent years, extended efforts in artificial cultivation have further expanded the range of established species in a multitude of glorious forms and colors. While most cultivated types found in Japan and other countries are hybrids of the original Chinese *Chrysanthemum Morifolium*, yet they vary so much from one to another that it is often difficult to perceive that they are even related.

Owing to the great variety of forms and shapes that the chrysanthemum has acquired through centuries of multifarious metamorphoses, the technical brushwork involved is more advanced. Although only four different types of plants are examined in this book, they represent the more popular genres embraced by artists through the ages. We will begin with the first type examined in the *Mustard Seed Garden Manual*, namely the flower with the "flat head and long petals."

The Flower with The "Flat Head and Long Petals"

To paint the petals, use a small firm brush such as the Leaf Vein brush illustrated in the Introduction. To start a flower with a large number of petals, a common feature of the chrysanthemum, begin with the few petals closest to the center, such as example E. Then insert the succeeding tiers of additional petals between those of the preceding layer (see the center column). However, this rule does not apply to buds, such as those on the right.

In general, most strokes move inward from the tip of the petal toward the center of the flower head (see arrows in A, B and D). Note that the stroke directions in C and E are optional and reversible.

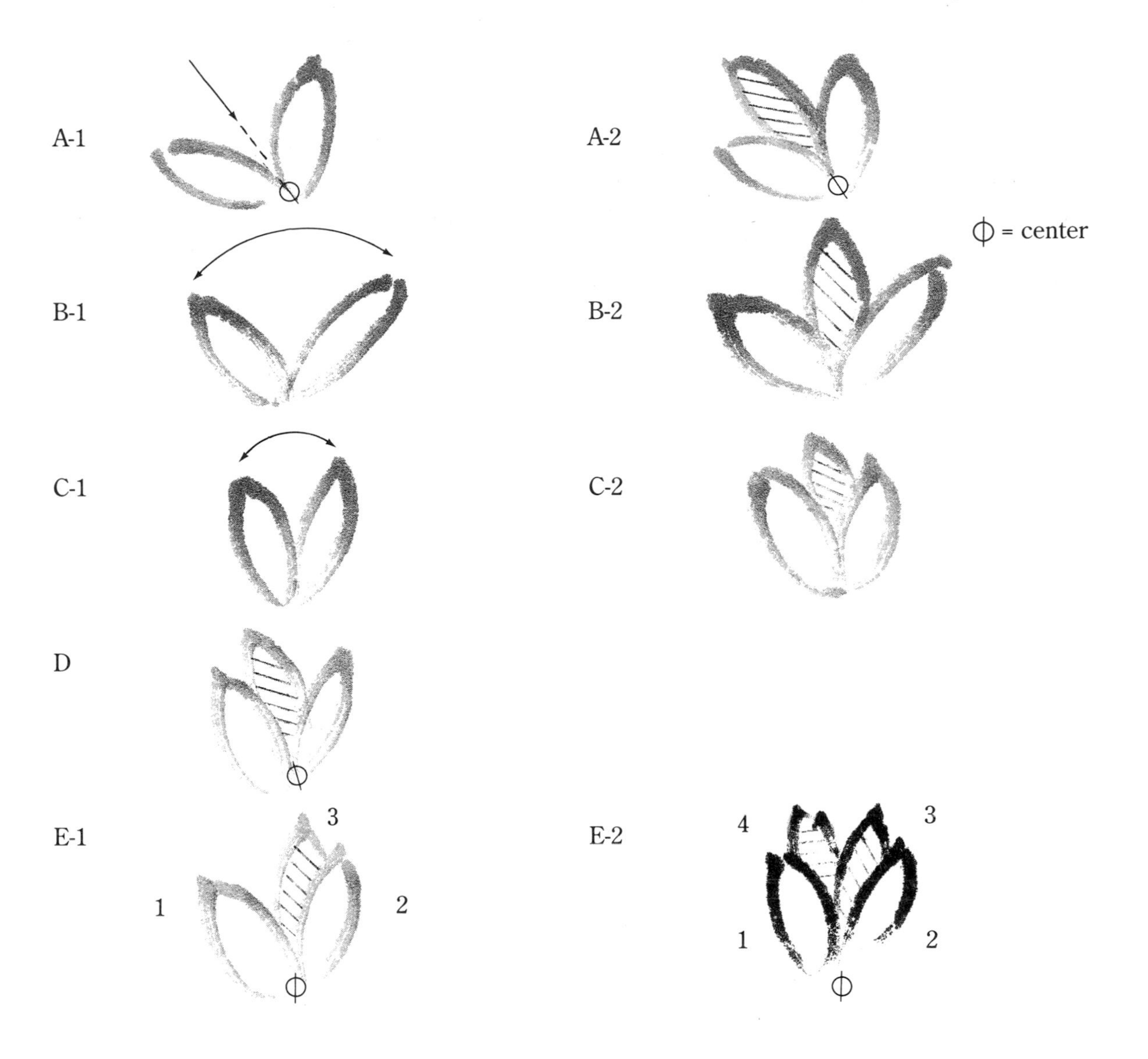

All stroke movements for the petals are directed at the core of the flower head. The same applies to the second-round inserts interposed between members of the initial group of six or so. (See arrows in A-1 and A-2. Examples B-2 and C-2 indicate that the rule applies in all instances, regardless of the area available for insertions.) When it is necessary to put in these inserts, lean to the left or to the right, to make room for a third round of petals on a higher level (example E-2). On petals set along the extreme perimeter, the two contour lines may not necessarily meet at the far end where a pointed tip is normally visible. The format is acceptable insofar as such petals are represented in the inclined position with the tips turned backward, in which case the top of the petals would be partly hidden from view.

The usual process of putting together a mature chrysanthemum flower begins with the correct placement of the center of the flower head around which the layers of petals sprout. As the flowers are basically round, the posture of a completed blossom would vary according to the position of that center within the circular form, as illustrated here. The center point is indicated by the dot inside the circles.

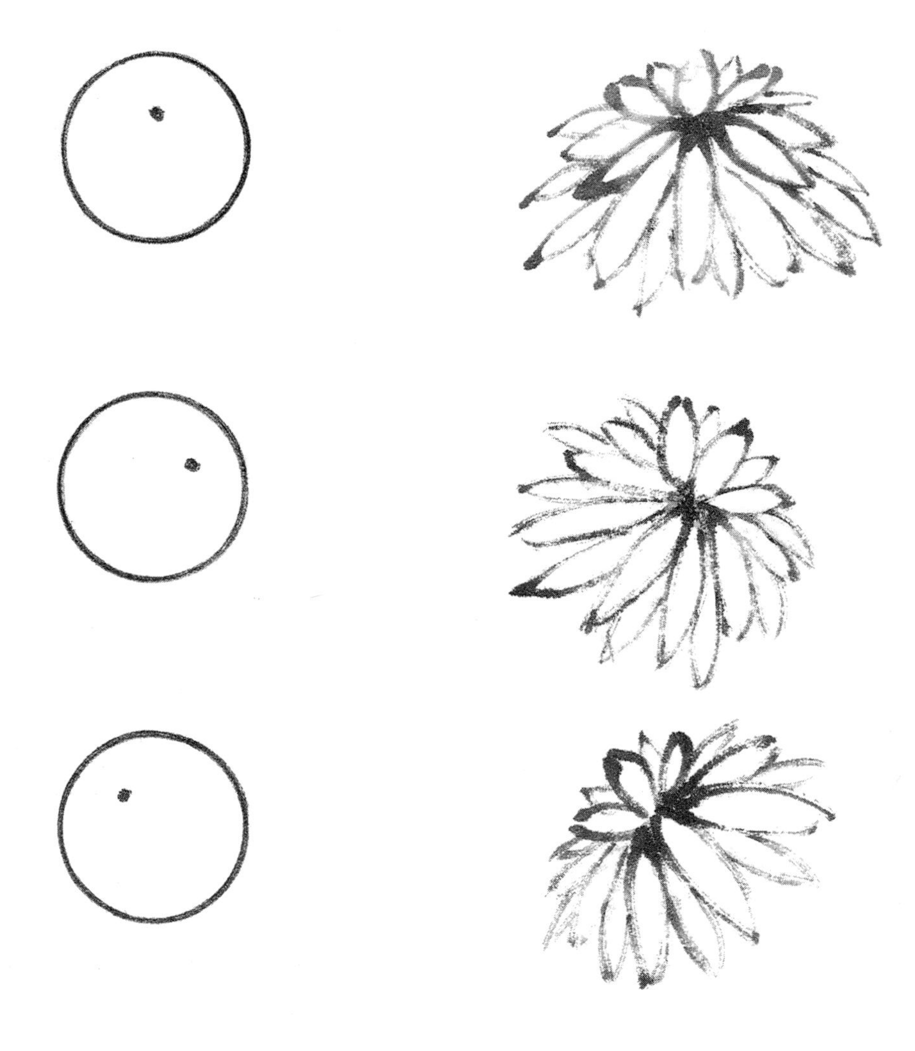

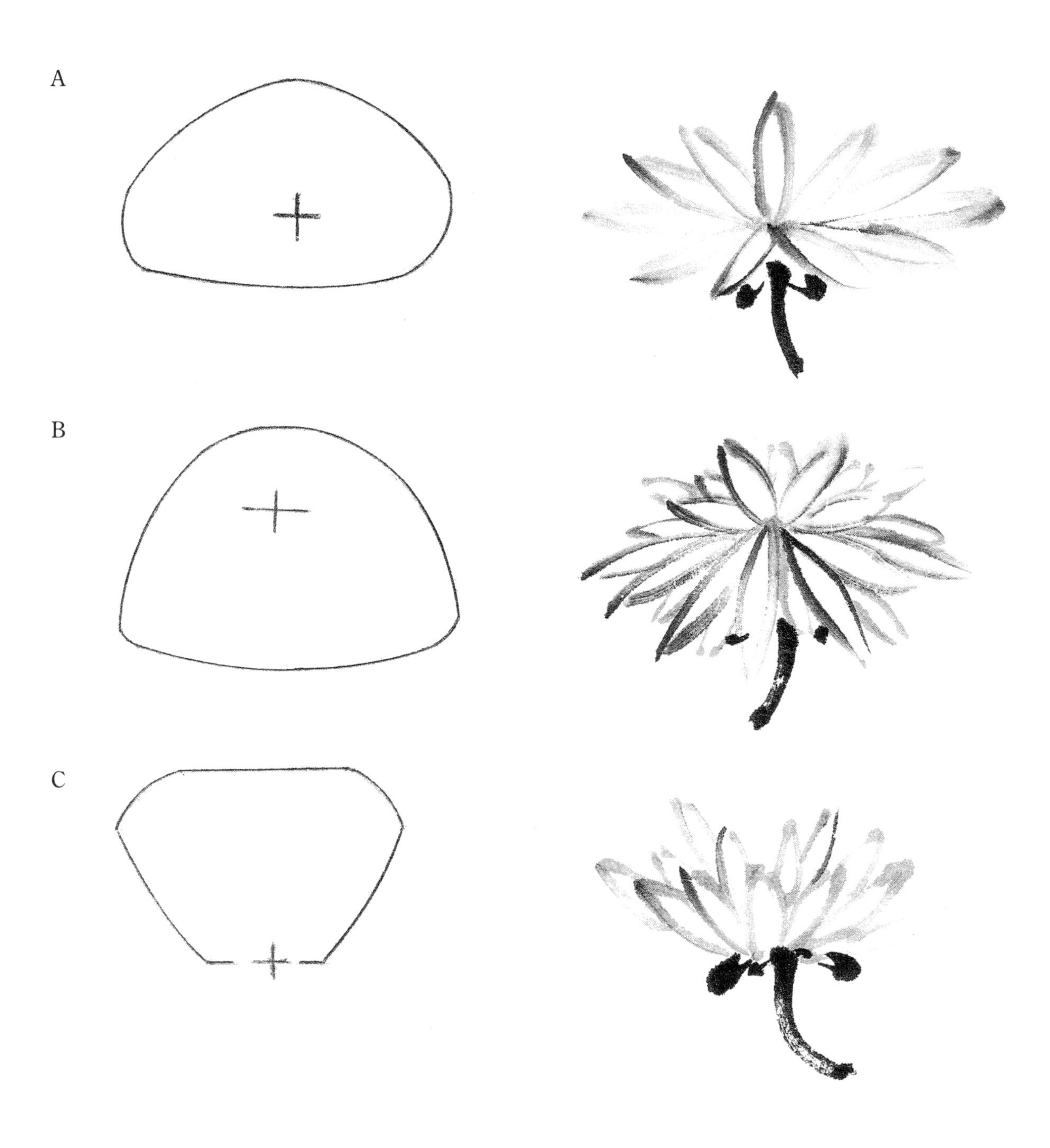

The small dots symbolizing the focal points illustrated in the preceding page are represented here by the crosses in examples A, B and C.

Chrysanthemum Leaves

Lateral Profiles in Three Strokes

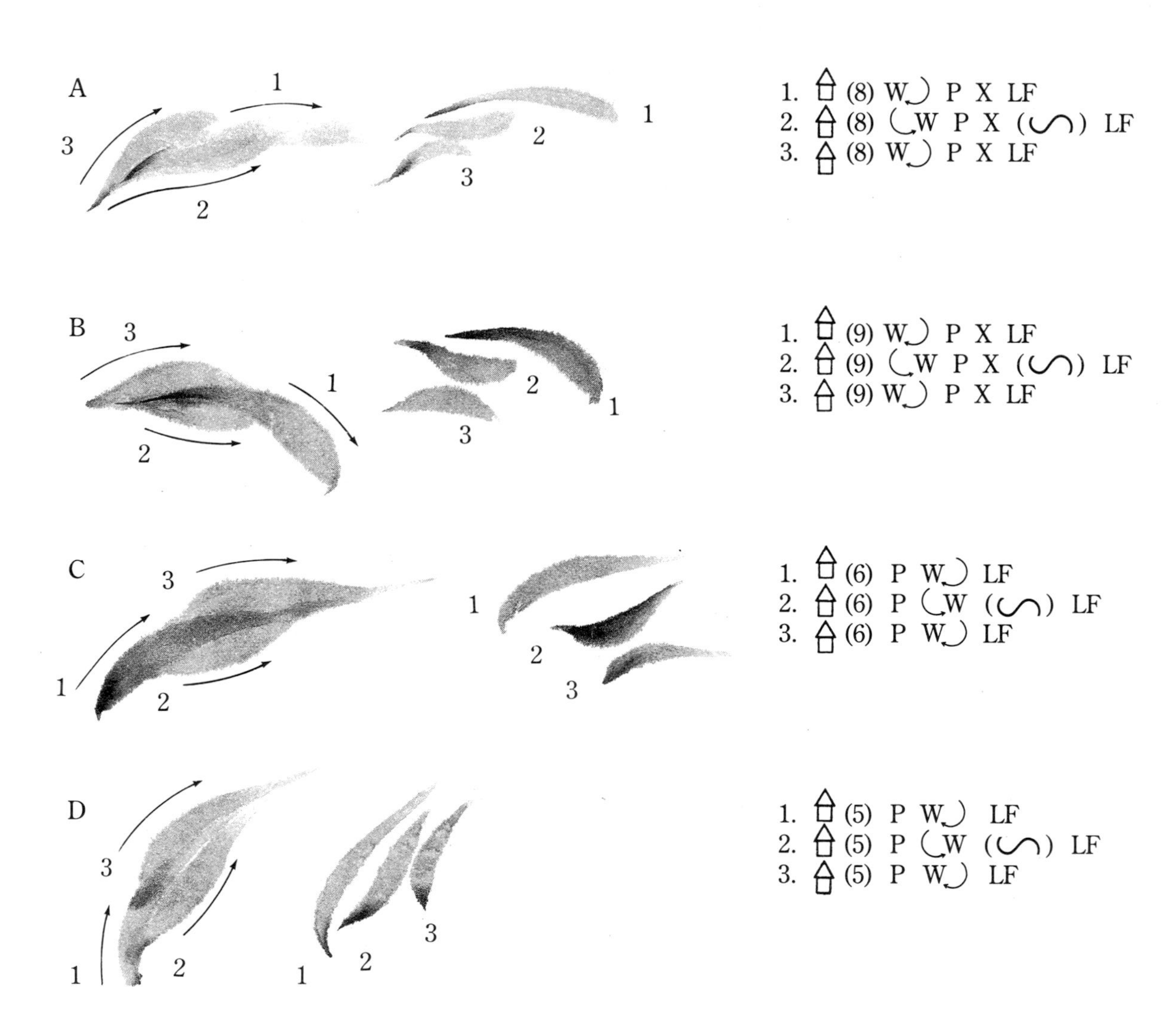

The sprightly dentate leaves of the chrysanthemum play an important supporting role in the painting of that flowering plant. On sidelong profiles of the lateral leaves, the upright hold is indispensable. Figures A, B, C and D are painted with a semi-dry, medium size Orchid-Bamboo brush charged with a medium load of light ink mixture. The letter "X" stands for a momentary pause prior to lift-off, and the symbol ∽ indicates the S-shaped turn on the second stroke.

Front View of Trifoliate Chrysanthemum Leaves (1)

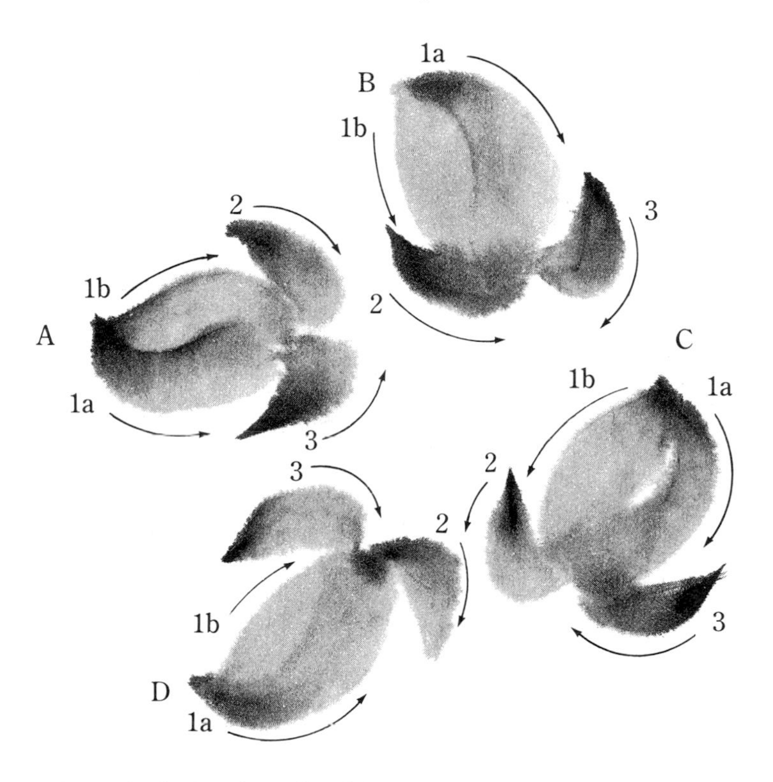

Details of brush strokes, clockwise from Leaf A:-

Leaf	Stroke	Details
A	1.a	(10) (W P BH
	1.b	(10) (W TH (∽)*
	2	(9) W) P BH
	3	(8) (W P BH
B	1.a	(9) W) P BH
	1.b	(9) (W TH (∽)
	2	(11) (W P BH
	3	(11) W) P BH
C	1.a	(11) W) P BH
	1.b	(11) (W TH (∽)
	2	(11) (W P BH
	3	(1) W) P BH
D	1.a	(9) (W P BH
	1.b	(9) (W TH (∽)
	2	(9) W) P BH LF
	3	(8) W) P BH LF

* The sign ∽ indicates an S-turn, in which the handle is shifted to the upright position to enable the tip to round out the S-curve after initial contact.

Trifoliate Chrysanthemum Leaves with Leaf Veins (2)

Notable points of general interest:

- All larger members of each cluster of three are drawn in two separate strokes.
- All strokes move from the tip toward the petioles, the leaf-stalks. (Exceptions to this rule are on the following page in a few examples of Leaves with Three to Five Leaflets (1) marked with arrows.)
- Collaborative movement of the lower arm is necessary on some of the more delicate S-turns, notably those occurring on one side of the contour lines shown in the preceding illustration.
- Double-loading of the brush tip is recommended for the purpose of highlighting the leaves.

Chrysanthemum Leaves with Three to Five Leaflets (1)

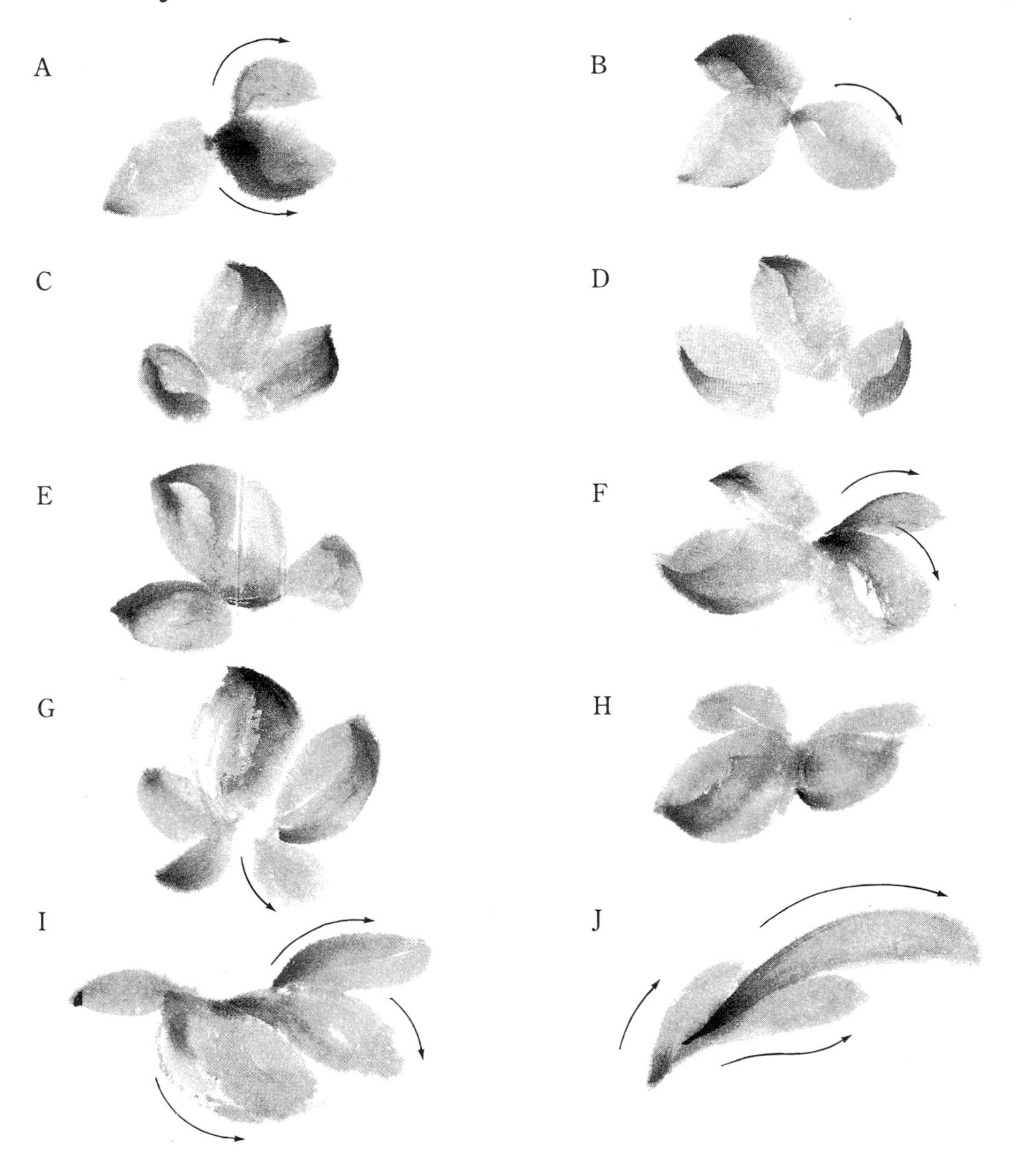

For matching examples with added leaf veins, see following page (AA, BB, etc.). Arrows indicate reverse strokes not begun at the tip of the leaves.

Chrysanthemum Leaves with Three to Five Leaflets and Added Leaf Veins (2)

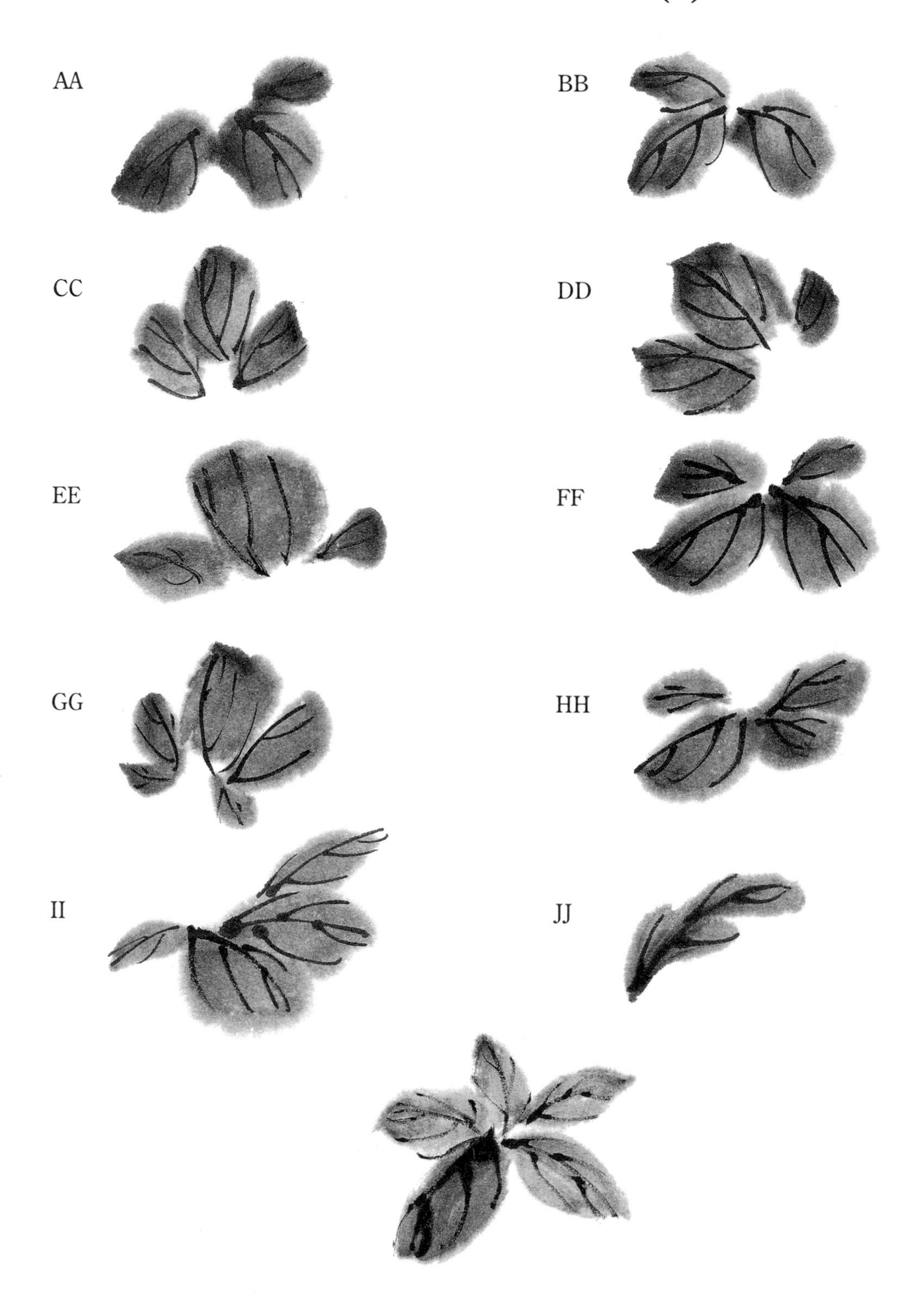

The Lithe Leaf Veins (1)

The Development of a Single Vein

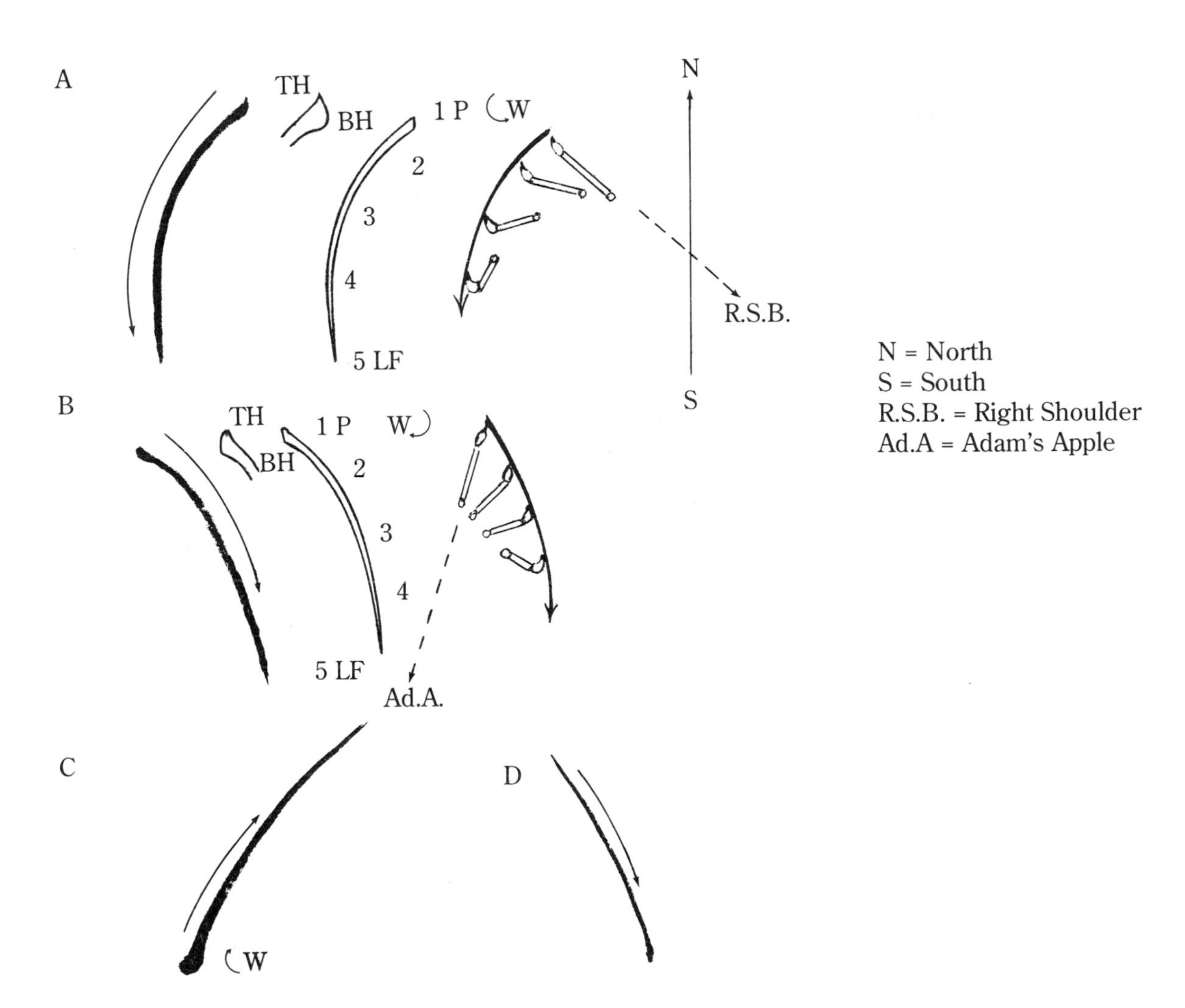

The chrysanthemum is often draped in a bountiful chemisette of dentate leaves that may outnumber the flowers by ten to one. The veins, by their lively ramifications, underscore the variegated posture of the leaves where they are placed in close quarters. Thus, the ability to draw the leaf veins in all their manifold forms as they infuse life to the flaccid leaves becomes in itself an important skill. The above diagrams provide a clearly-defined system of practice by plotting the step-by-step progression of the formation of curved, yet tactile, strokes. (Further explanation on the following page.)

Explanatory Notes on the Step-by-Step Formation of a Leaf Vein *

Example A

Step 1

Here the brush is set down with tip (TH) pointing to 11 o'clock. (A magnified head section is placed next to Example A to show the relative positions between TH and BH at this point. Normally, the distance of the two is seldom greater than 1/16 to 1/8 of an inch.) The lower position of the BH denotes the oblique posture of the handle at the beginning where pressure (P) is briefly applied. In the third column four brushes represent the four stages of brushstroke movement alongside an arc similar to Example A. Further down, the letters "R.S.B." stand for Right Shoulder Blade, which indicates the approximate height of the top of the handle at the point where it is first set down on the paper. The positions of the four brushes correspond to the four points marked 1 to 4 on the outlined example shown in the third column. Step 1 ends with a momentary pause following the application of pressure.

Step 2

Step 2 begins with the wrist turning in an anti-clockwise direction, with the hand simultaneously directing the brush to move in the southwesterly direction along the arc. Up to this point, the elbow remains in a fixed position, acting as the fulcrum for the lower arm. The hand, too, has to turn with the wrist in order to hold the brush down on the paper. Meanwhile, the hand is also engaged in shifting the handle to a more upright position, to slim down the width of the vein after the stroke leaves the head section where it is connected with the petiole. From here on, uniformity of width is secured by maintaining a constant level of height of the brush in motion. The low end of the handle should also advance to a forward position to stay abreast of the rest of the brush so that the hairs are bent backward throughout the stroke. (See posture of brush no. 2 in diagram.)

Step 3

Since it is the rotating motion of the wrist that brings about the elevation of the handle to a higher position, it follows that, once the circular track moves beyond the peak of the loop, the handle will begin its descent in the opposite direction somewhere around position 3 in the diagram. The elbow is now unlocked from its original position to allow the hand to proceed further without hindrance.

Step 4

From this point onward, the course enters upon its last and comparatively straight sector. During the closing stages of the brushstroke, it is of extreme

* The explanations above refer to the examples illustrated on the preceding page under "The Lithe Leaf Vein (1), The Development of a Single Vein."

importance that the tip of the brush is kept at the center of the stroke in preparation for the final lift-off from the paper.

Finally, where effective brushwork control is concerned, the wrist is the one that provides the motive energy necessary in the direction of the upright brush.

Example B

Step 1

Action begins with the tip pointing roughly in the same direction as Example A, i.e., 12 o'clock. However, there is one important difference. While in Example A, the palm in the opening position is turned to the left toward approximately 10 o'clock, the palm here is turned downward toward the tabletop. Further, where the top of the handle in Example A points at the Right Shoulder Blade, that part of the handle will now be aligned with the Adam's Apple. This is particularly so if the vein happens to be in the center, or left of center, of the painting surface. (Once again, this is a rough approximation for a right-handed person.) Apart from these two differences, other stroking requirements are basically the same except that the directions of the movements are reversed. Where the line moves toward the left in Example A, now the general direction is toward the right, etc.

Step 2

One important technical difference between A and B happens in this area. For the movement of the brush in the southeasterly direction is mainly regulated by the middle and fourth fingers as the stroke starts to move away from the petiole assisted by the wrist turning in the clockwise direction. Once again, moving the brush away from the point of contact with the wrist in a fixed position, would tend to reduce the width of the stroke. On the other hand, the movement here is more restricted because of the shorter mobile range of the fingers compared to that of the entire hand in the other case. Here the tendency is for the brush to be pulled back after a short distance and to veer toward a more southerly direction.

Step 3

Here the whole arm is moved back so as not to block the movement of the brush going in the direction of 5 o'clock, particularly if the stroke is a long one. As in the case of the drooping bamboo leaves moving in that direction, here too, the elbow may have to be raised as the arm is pulled back where the subject matter is located near the bottom of the paper.

Steps 4 & 5

The same ground rules for Example A are applicable in general, except that the compass points should be suitably modified.

Example C

In many ways this is Example A in reverse, except for the following differences:

1. The direction of the tip pointing at 8 o'clock at the point of impact.
2. Unlike Example A, the palm at Step 1 is turned in the direction of 9 o'clock.
3. The turn of the wrist is in the clockwise direction.

In general, this is an easier stroke than the other three examples. There are none of the restrictive elements to curb the hand from moving freely throughout the course from beginning to end.

Example D

This is a true "reverse" stroke in the sense that the action begins not from the petiole of the leaf, but from the small end of it, much as in the case of the orchid petals. This truly facilitates the stroking motions. The example here is drawn entirely with the upright brush. A slight slant to the left would produce a wider vein at the middle section.

Finally, there is no left or right turn of the wrist involved in this type of brushwork and all that it does is to allow the hand to make a slightly curved lateral motion in a co-ordinated action supported by all parts of the arm, even the shoulder blade.

The Lithe Leaf Veins (2)

Brushstroke Order and Changing Profiles

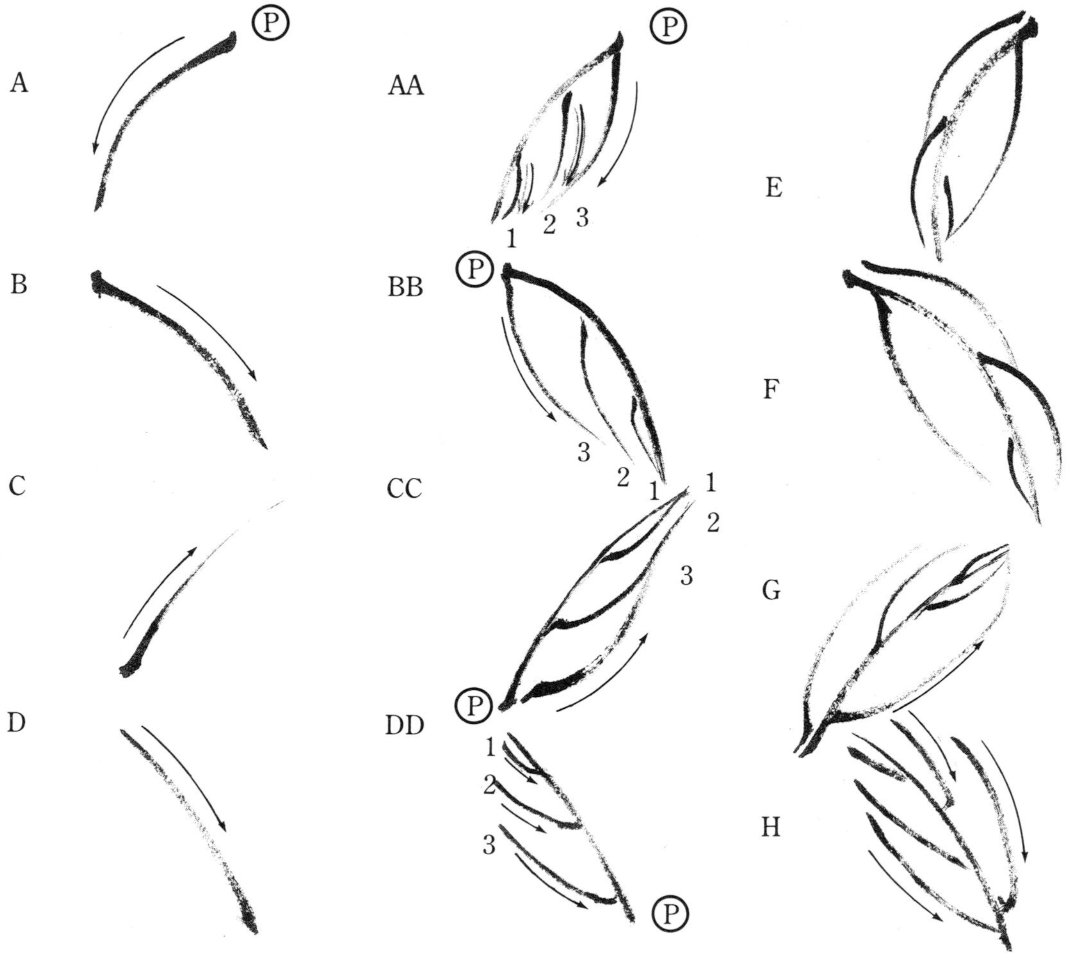

The Leaf Vein brush is specially designed for drawing leaf veins. Except for Example D, or the center veins of DD and H, all strokes begin with a brief pause (P). In the case of D and DD, etc., the pressure is applied at the end. Where pressure is exerted at the beginning, it is gradually released as the brush is shifted to the upright position for the line to assume a sharp point at the very end. The arrows indicate the direction of the stroke movement while the numbers alongside the shorter veins (second column) represent the order in which these are added. The same order applies to the lateral veins in Examples E, F, G and H which represent frontal profiles seen from a different angle. Here too, you start with the shortest one at the top.

As a rule, the veins are filled in only after the body wash—or, in the case of the outlined mode, the body contour lines—is in place. Consequently, a darker ink mixture for the veins is essential. If body wash is used, such as in the examples on the following pages, the leaf veins must be brought in when the wash is approximately 85% dry.

The Chrysanthemum (1)

Flat Head and Long Pointed Petals

Details of Flowers F1 and F2

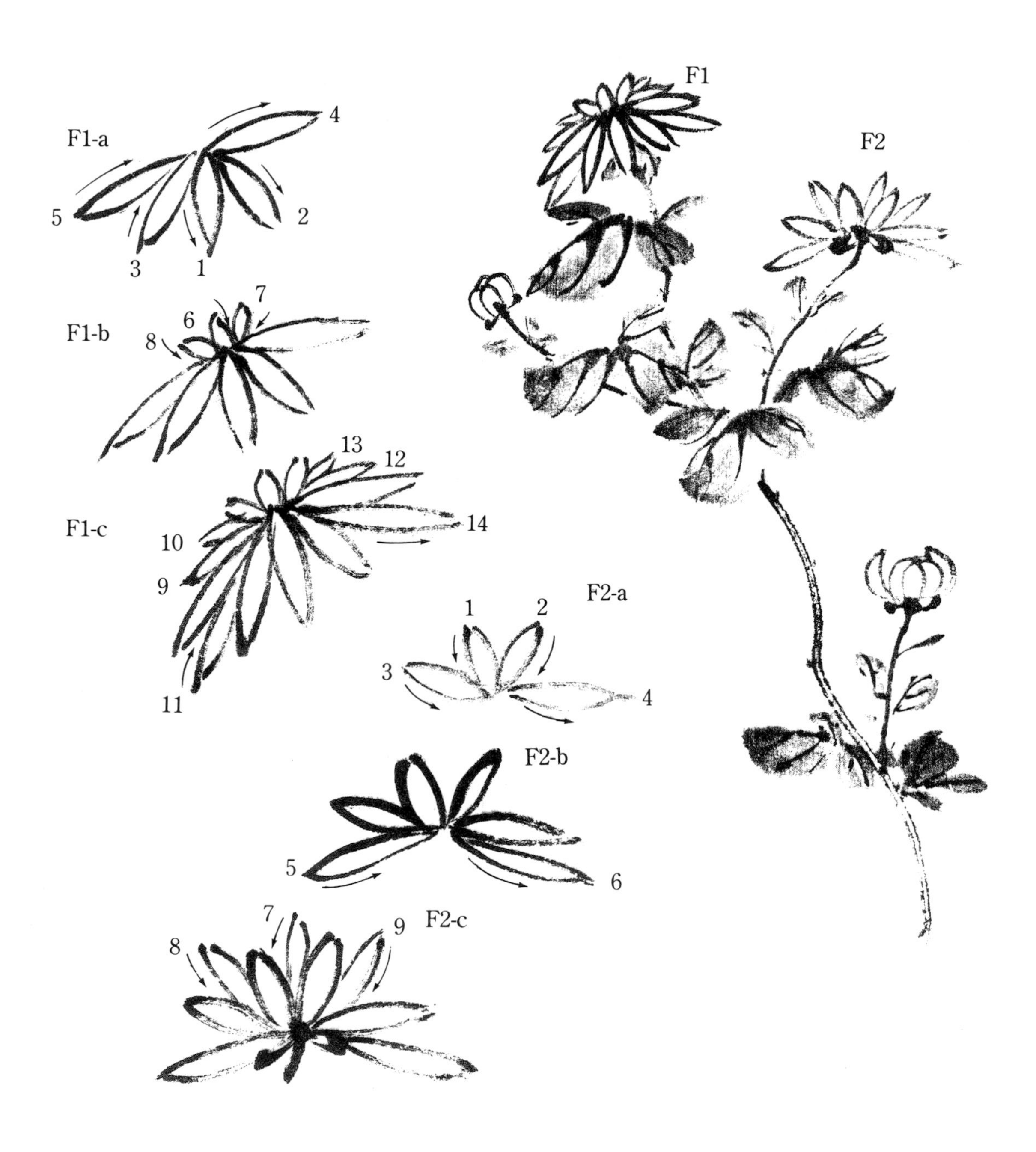

Numbers represent sequence of drawing. Arrows indicate brushstroke directions.

The Steps in The Development of A Complete Plant

The Chrysanthemum (2)

Compact Flat Head, Short Petals and Top Disk of Stamens and Pistils

Changing The Profiles of Composite Chrysanthemum Flower Heads

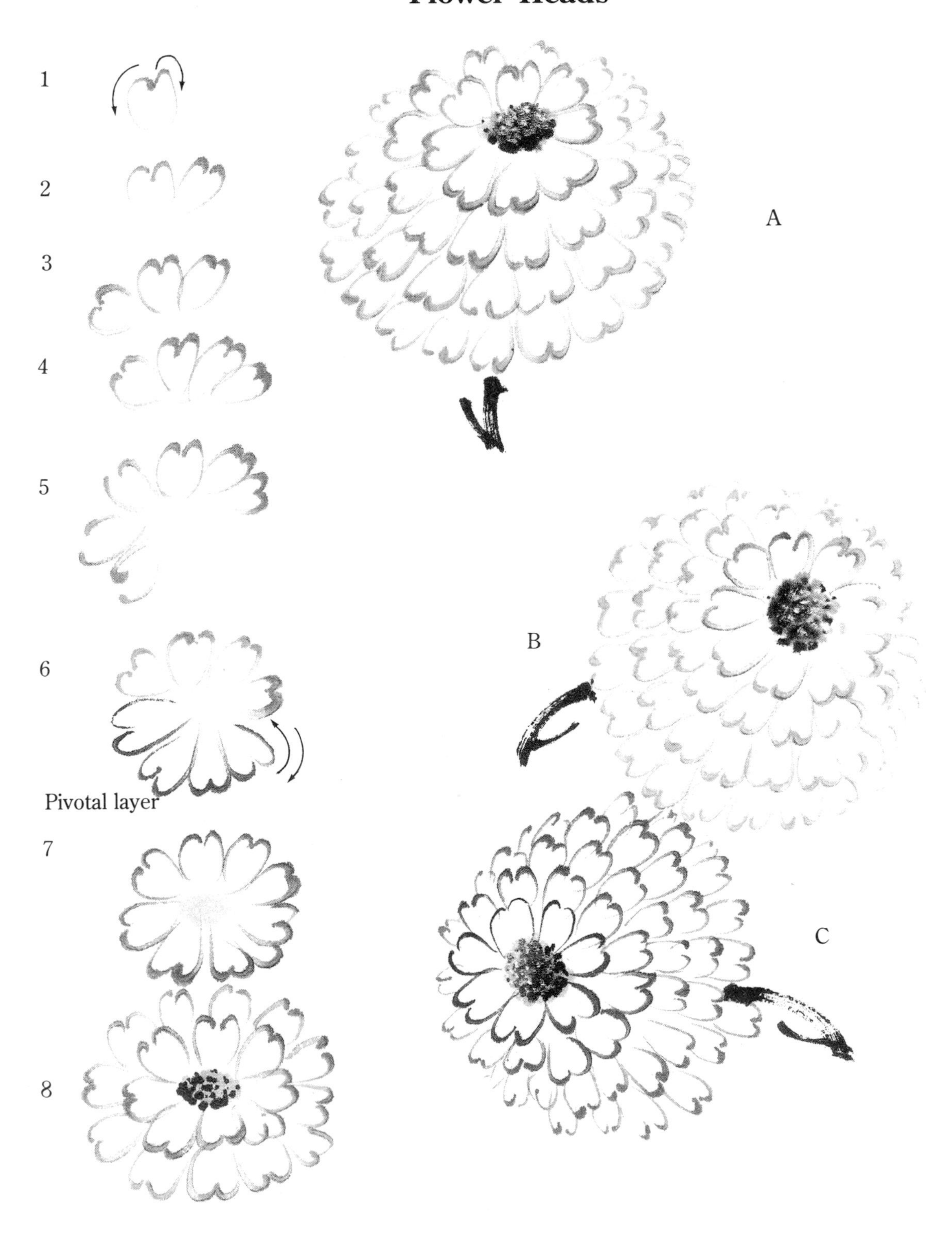

Explanatory notes on changing the profiles of composite flower heads

Because of the large number of petals present in a composite chrysanthemum flower head, the medium size Orchid-Bamboo brush containing an ample ink reservoir in the belly is well suited for our purpose since adequate carrying capacity allows a uniform color tone to be maintained without the need for too frequent reloading. Following is a list of useful guidelines on the technical process of composing compact chrysanthemum flower heads:

1. Begin by loading the brush with a light-medium mixture up to three-quarters of the length of the tuft, followed by a second loading of a darker mixture up to one-eighth of an inch.

2. All strokes begin from the curved end of the line and curve inward as indicated by the arrows in Example 1. (Note the exception illustrated by the counter-moving arrows in Example 6, indicating that either direction is possible.)

3. Action opens with the tip of the brush pointing straight down at the center of the curved loop—i.e. the top part of the two separate strokes in Example 1—but without actually touching it. With the wrist locked in position, lower the brush to draw the loop by rolling the wrist in the direction indicated by the arrows and working the handle of the brush the way a free pointed branch works in a pair of compasses. (See blank area of outlined example below.) The second and last

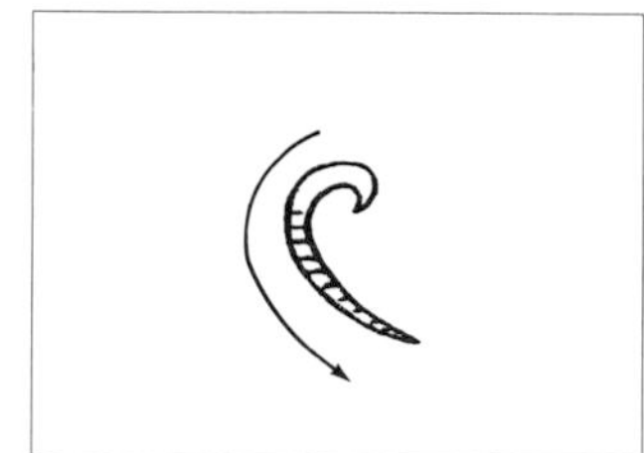

part of the stroke—shaded area—is executed by hunching the wrist upward with middle and fourth fingers working together to steer the brush in the direction of the center of the flower head. The brush should be held firmly by the hand while a co-ordinated backward movement of the lower arm may be necessary toward the end prior to lift-off depending on the length of the stroke.

4. The first task is to complete the first pivotal ring all round the circular flower head (see Example 6). After that, the mode of distribution of the rest of the petals along succeeding layers may deviate from the format initially applied, and may actually develop into a variety of lopsided, asymmetrical patterns peculiar to the particular posture of the flower in specific positions. In Example A, which is shown in the upright position, there are only two layers of petals at the top against five at the bottom. By changing the patterns of distribution of the petals of Examples B and C around the same pivotal area, it is possible to drastically alter the postures of these two

blossoms so that the former now faces the right while the other is turned 90° toward the left. It is therefore advisable to have a good idea of the posture of the completed product before you start to fill in the petals on the lower levels below the first layer.

5. Finally, as in most other situations, the upright brush is essential when painting scores of delicate chrysanthemum petals which have to be strung together in good order within a small, compact area. But do not attempt to do a whole flower head until, through practice, you are fairly competent at coping with all the metastatic postures of each and every petal of a composite group over a wide range of the circumference.

6. In Example 7, a dilute ink mixture is used to delineate the center area of the flower head. The dots representing the stamens are added at random in dark ink (see Example 8, etc.) before the light mixture in Example 7 has dried up completely. The dots are not of equal size and are not evenly distributed so as to highlight the uneven surface of the whole area.

The Chrysanthemum (2)
Compact Flower Head and Short Petals

Compact Chrysanthemum Flowers

1

X

Y

2

3

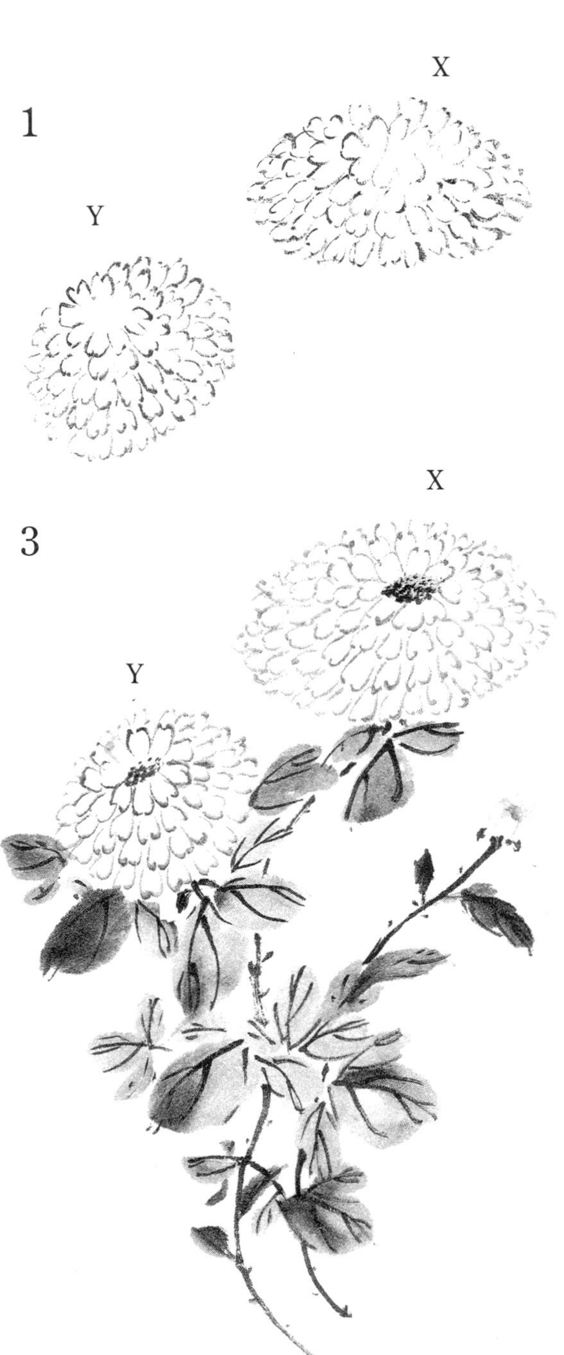

The Steps in Organizing a Simple Composition

1. Placement of the dominant subjects; in this case the two flower heads X and Y set the shape of later developments.
2. While the two flowers at the top reflect an air of princely elegance, the leaves on the other hand seem to sway from side to side as if they were about to take off. Here the fluttering leaves waltzing down from the base of flower head Y along the line of the stems complete the pattern of the inverted letter "L" marked by the three points X, Y and Z.
3. The small bud on the right in an otherwise blank area is a favorite second-string subject of interest in traditional paintings of the chrysanthemum. Here it sets off by counter-point the inclination of flower head Y in the opposite direction.

   Now is the time to bring in the stems, or portions of them glimpsed from between the leaves, together with the branches and a number of desultory, ancillary leaves.

   From this point onward you change to a darker ink mixture to fill in the veins on the leaves and dot the center of the flower heads to highlight the stamens. Finally, the lobes on the stems and branches are dabbed on at random.

The Boneless* Chrysanthemum

* Ibid "*Mo-ku* Boneless" petals in "The Plum."

Boneless Chrysanthemum Petals

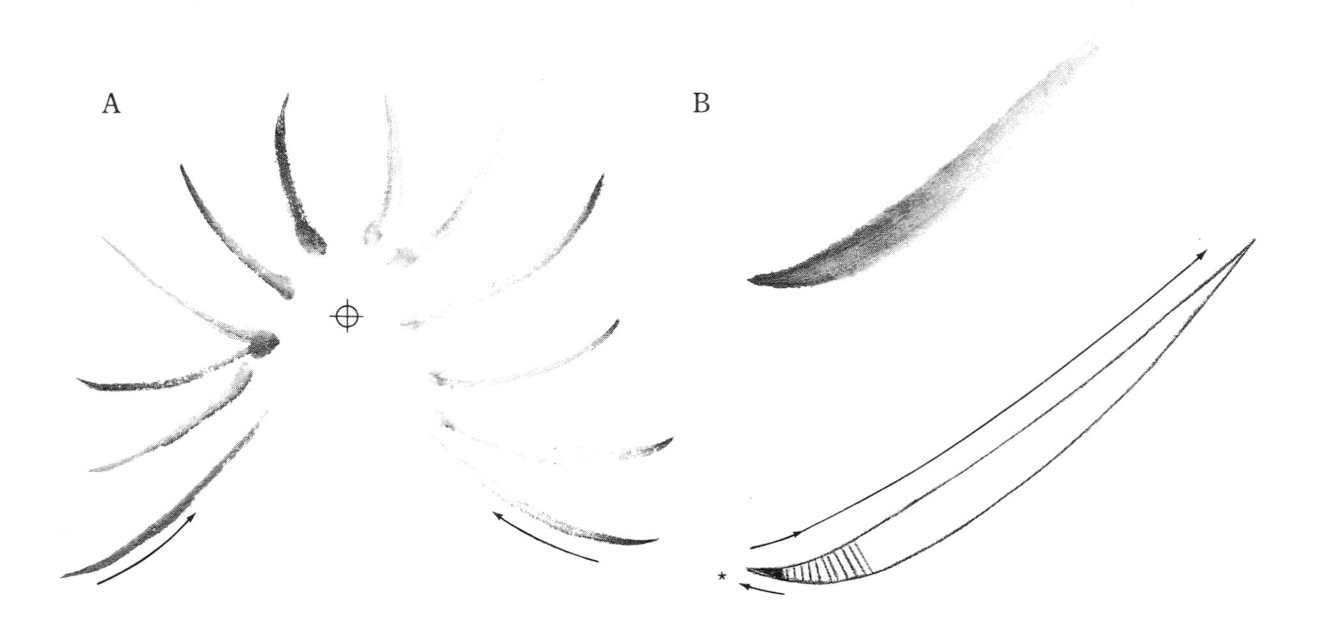

All strokes begin from the tip and terminate at the center area indicated by the sign ⊕ in Fig. A. (The configuration of the drooping crown shown here is compressed for lack of space.)

A right-handed person drawing the petals on the lower right side of Fig. A would sometimes find it necessary to shift the paper to the side in order to free the wrist from having to operate the brush upward in a cramped situation.

The outlined example of a petal in Fig. B is divided into three separate sections—black, shaded and white. To hold the tip pointing ahead at a low slant, which is essential in the formation of a sharp needle point at the very outset (small arrow in black area), the hand has to be hunched back all the way against the wrist.

The change of direction in the shaded area is regulated mainly by the wrist turning to the left or right depending on whether

* Arrow indicates the direction in which the tip is set prior to making contact with the paper.

the petal is situated on the right or left side of the profile of the flower. In the example the turn is to the right CW.

Because there is a limit to the way in which the wrist is capable of turning in either direction, and further, because such limit is directly related to the opening position of the tip of the brush as it is set down initially, great care should be exercised to check out the projected route of the white area each time before you set the tip down on the paper to start painting.

A second role of the wrist is to apply a brief pressure on the brush to widen the contour of the line as illustrated, which serves the dual function of signaling to the painter through increased friction that the moment is ripe to head straight into the targeted course over the white area. Further on, the whole arm must join in the action.

Finally, along with the changes in the technical aspects of the three areas, these may as well be divided into three different rhythmic zones:

Black area – slow
Shaded area – slower
White area – sustained moderate speed increasing to controlled vivacity at the end.

Putting Together A Chrysanthemum Flower of The "Boneless" Mode (Type 3)

The type of brushwork involved in drawing the "boneless" chrysanthemum is in many ways analogous to that indicated earlier for the "boneless" orchid petals. Once again, the strokes start at the tip of the petal to terminate at the base around the perimeter of the pedicel. The numbers 1 to 16 alongside the petals in diagrams A, B and C indicate the order of painting the petals in the development of the completed flower head shown as Example D.

This process is given for purpose of study only, since flowers of other shapes and dimensions may require altogether different structural designs.

As noted, there are altogether 16 petals of varying forms and lengths in the third diagram, each sprouting in divergent directions. The preferred order of painting would be to approach them from two different directions one side at a time in separate groups to ensure ease of operation by the wrist, which is crucial in this type of brushwork. However, this consideration does not apply to the insertion of desultory petals once the initial framework is in place.

Details of all four diagrams are as follows:

A

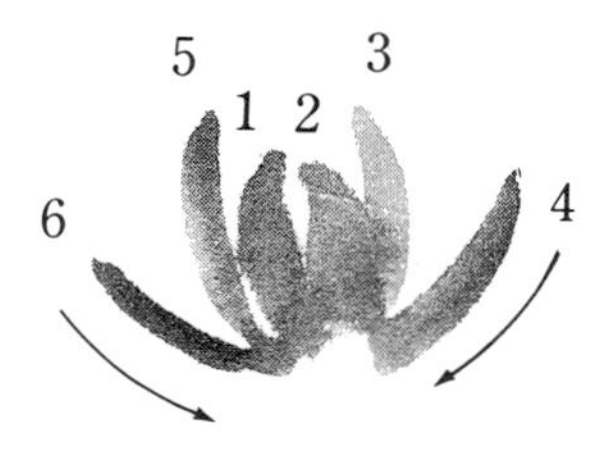

A. Contrary to the rule of alternate side painting mentioned above, the first two petals are always taken together in sequence to mark the center line between the two sides and, more importantly, to serve as the arrowhead which sets the general direction in which the whole mushrooming structure will eventually develop.

B

B. Note the gaps left between the petals into which additional petals will be inserted at the next round of floral building. For petals in the background, a diluted ink mixture is effective in providing color tone contrast to heighten the sense of depth.

C

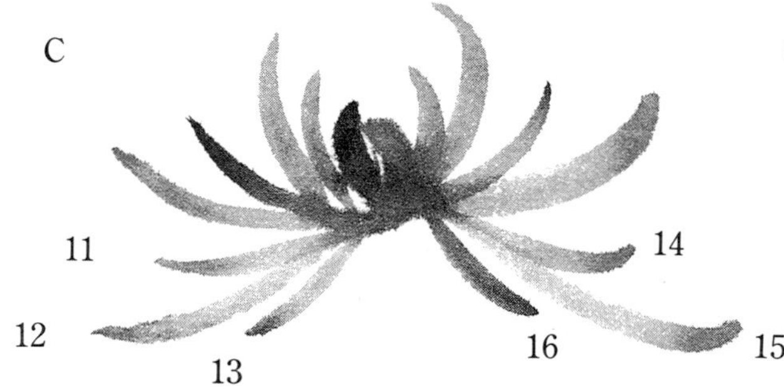

C. As you come down the two sides of the dome-shaped profile of a mature blossom, the long and drooping petals would not be as dense as those appearing around the center where new growths are continuously sprouting.

D

D. After diagram C, the stage is set to bring in a few select petals in staggered lengths and curvatures as necessary to avoid any appearance of contrived, stereotyped execution.

The Boneless Chrysanthemum (3)

The Story Behind The Development of A Painting of The Chrysanthemum (Type 3)

1

1. As usual the principal subjects are taken care of first because this is the only time the artist can place them anywhere he pleases over a completely blank piece of paper. However, before you move on to the next phase of painting, be sure to fill in the sepals and a short length of the top section of the pedicel to ensure that the color tone between the flowers and these parts would merge perfectly at the joints.

2

2. Next to be set down are the clusters of primary leaves which are to be painted only after you have mapped out in your mind the projected line of the stems from the ground up. Here, four separate clusters are set in their respective stations to block the large number of closely meandering branches criss-crossing between the two stems, as well as to break up the long spindly shafts of the latter which, if unchecked, would draw attention away from the flowers as the premier elements of the painting.

3

3. With the primary leaves in place, part of the stems may now be extended down to the perimeters of the first clusters of leaves in their path. To the left, a bud peering out from the encasement of guardian leaves sets off the elegant forms of two mature blossoms, their heads held high in regal probity. And the addition of a single swaying leaf at the far left completes the image of the swirling skirts of two dancers cutting pirouettes in the autumn breeze.

4

4. The last cluster of leaves should be attended to before the two stems are joined up with their stumps at the bottom. The insertion at random of the small, rudimentary leaves and the lobes of the branches completes the picture.

The Curly Chrysanthemum

The Making of A Curly Chrysanthemum Petal

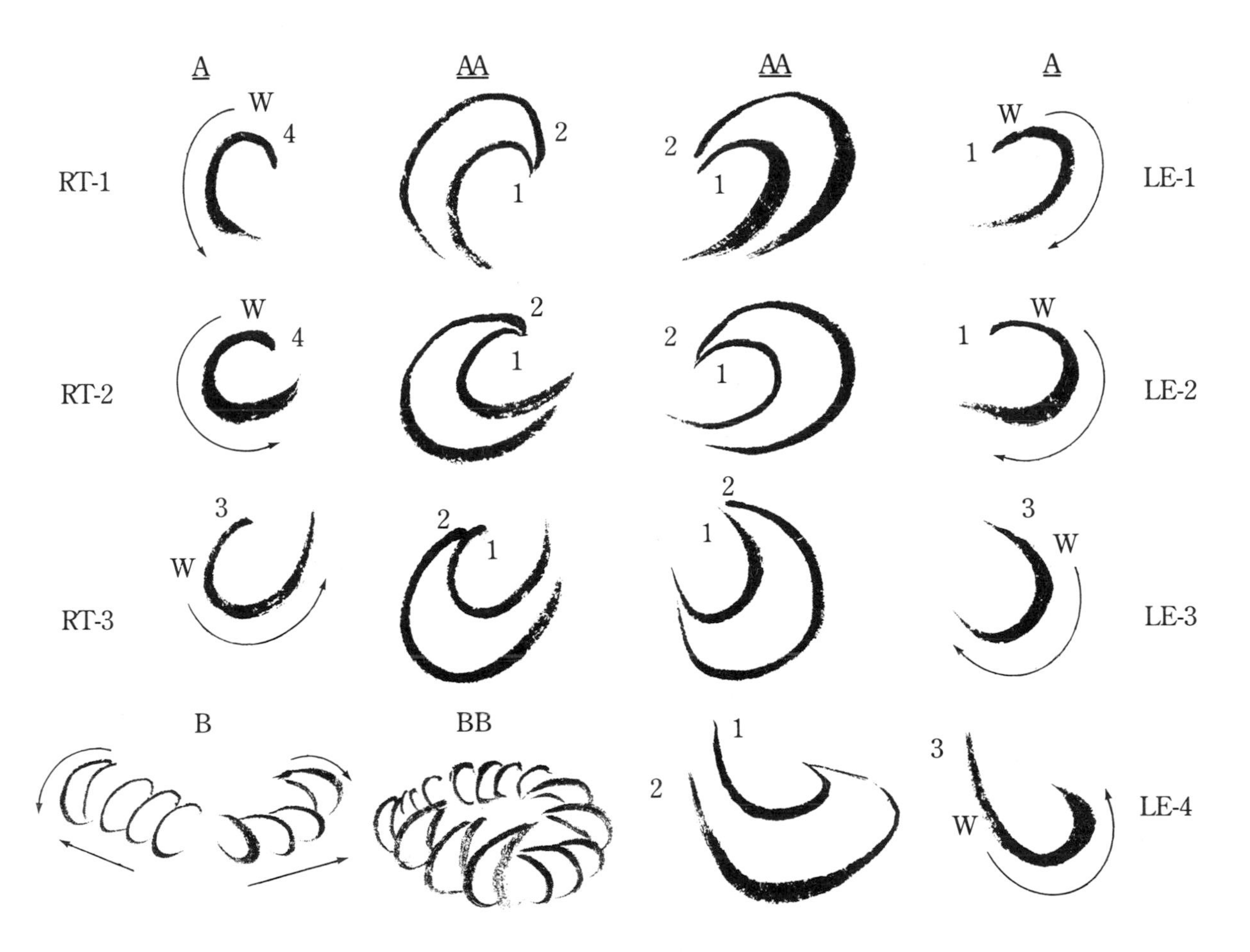

RT	=	Stroke ending to the right
LE	=	Stroke ending to the left
A	=	Inside loop
AA	=	Second loop added to form a spiraling curly petal
B	=	Type of strokes commonly used to depict the neck around the flower head
BB	=	Example of completed neck

Pressure either in the form of BP-1 or BP-2, once initiated, should be kept up until shortly before the tip is lifted off the paper.
A relaxed and supple wrist regulating the brush in the upright position is indispensable in this type of manipulative brushwork.

Details of brushstrokes on the curly chrysanthemum petals

The numbers 1, 3 and 4 under the two columns marked A in the diagrams illustrated on the preceding page represent the fingers that play a significant role in steering the brush at the beginning of each stroke. Further on, the progress of the brush is directed solely by the action of the wrist. The beginning of this section is indicated by the combined symbol "W→." Where the length of a stroke is such that it exceeds the maximum operative radius of the wrist, then the lower arm has to be involved to extend the range.

Of the two spiraling helical lines that form the head of the curly petals, the inner loop is set down first in order to provide greater manipulative freedom for the hand to work upon inserting the exterior line over and around the smaller loop, as indicated by the numbers 1 and 2 in examples illustrated under the two columns marked AA.

As a rule, drawing the svelte loops of the petals requires a firm grip on the handle of the brush at all times. Other pre-requisites include the co-ordination of a flexible wrist supported by a relaxed arm and hand working the brush in the upright position. And lastly use only the top portion of the few longest hairs at the tip of the tuft lightly charged with moderately dark ink.

In addition, both lines of the helical loops should be laid down deliberately and with a measure of controlled celerity. Reduced pace is recommended only for the following two areas: (1) at the beginning of the stroke before the sign "W→," and (2) around the area where the line is about to uncurl prior to proceeding onto the final straight section terminating at the rim of the flower head. In this last section, a conscious effort has to be made by the wrist to direct the brush to head toward the flower head even before the loop is completely unwound.

Finally, the shape of a complete curly petal may be affected by any one of the following causes:

A. The direction in which the tip of the brush is pointed at the start of the stroke. (In general, starting a stroke with the tip pointing in the direction of the center of the flower head would correctly preset the length of the curved portion of a curlicue so that, as the brush approaches the end of the loop, it is programed to begin the turn into the last sector at the correct spot to head straight for its final targeted position.)

B. The angle of the lower arm. (This varies according to the opening position cited in A.)

C. The height of the hand hold on the handle of the brush. (This determines the size of the spiraling loop.)

The steps in organizing an interlocking tress of curly chrysanthemum petals

The oval rings around the four letters A, B, C and D represent the area at the pedicel from which the petals sprout and fan out in all directions. The order of painting the curlicues is exemplified by the series of four figures marked A to D as shown. It will be noted that only half a profile is illustrated so that, after studying it, the student may experiment with filling out the other half before trying his hand on his own complete model. There are of course other ways of setting up a curly chrysanthemum flower.

A

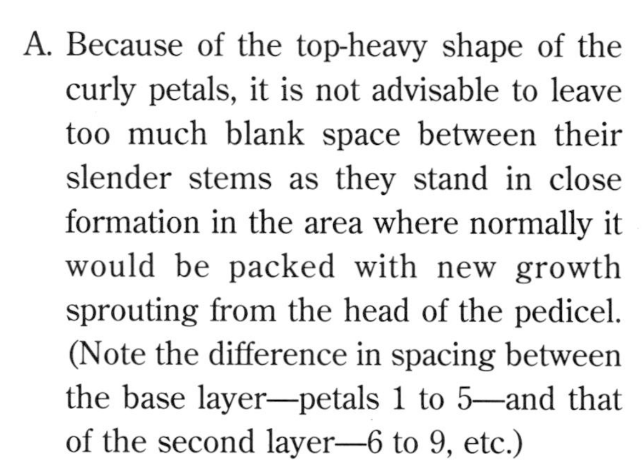

A. Because of the top-heavy shape of the curly petals, it is not advisable to leave too much blank space between their slender stems as they stand in close formation in the area where normally it would be packed with new growth sprouting from the head of the pedicel. (Note the difference in spacing between the base layer—petals 1 to 5—and that of the second layer—6 to 9, etc.)

B

B. On the insertion of a new round of curlicues over the preceding layer, attention should be given to the need for threading their tail ends through the circlets of the petals immediately beneath them. Before setting the brush down to start a new curlicue make sure it is correctly postured so that the way the threading is executed would not appear to be unnaturally affected as a result of having to maneuver the tip of the brush within very close quarters. (By going right through between two of the lower petals without threading, no. 8 as shown is the exception to the rule to provide occasional relief against the uniformity of the motif.)

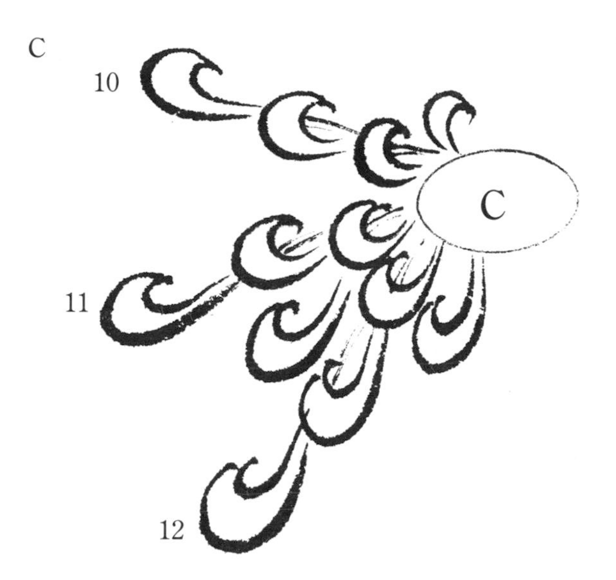

C. The insertion and placement of the few longer petals are of exceptional importance because of the conspicuous position they occupy standing with heads and shoulders above the rest of the ensemble.

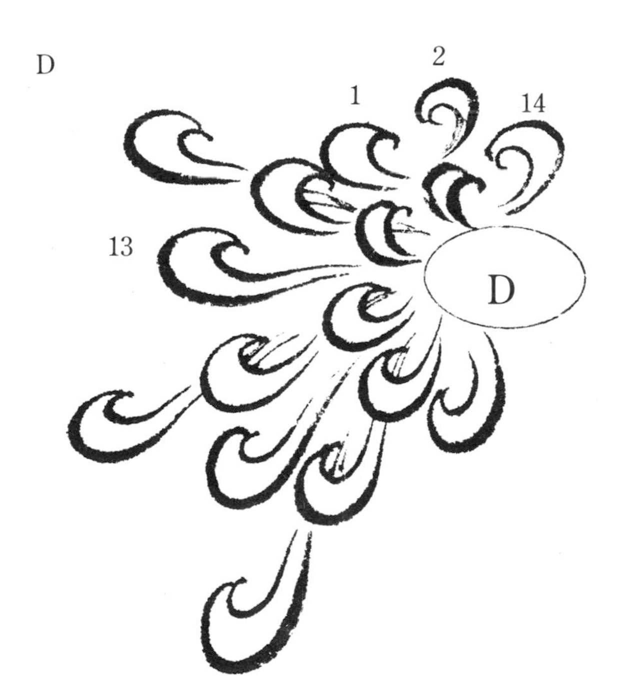

D. At this stage, additional petals are introduced at random as necessary. When one side of the tress is done, start at the top again on the first inverse curlicue at the opposite side represented by petal 14. The two odd petals marked 1 and 2 next to 14 can be filled in at the very last moment, or whenever there is need to build up the profile of the crown to set off the large number of those ranged along the lateral sides. Note that petal no. 13 is another exception to the rule—the space left open between 10 and 11 now pervaded by a single long petal fulfilling the same function as 8 in B.

The Curly Chrysanthemum

INDEX